Approaches to learning and teaching

Modern Foreign Languages

a toolkit for international teachers

**Series Editors and Authors:
Paul Ellis and Lauren Harris**

CAMBRIDGE
UNIVERSITY PRESS

University Printing House, Cambridge CB2 8BS, United Kingdom

One Liberty Plaza, 20th Floor, New York, NY 10006, USA

477 Williamstown Road, Port Melbourne, VIC 3207, Australia

314–321, 3rd Floor, Plot 3, Splendor Forum, Jasola District Centre, New Delhi – 110025, India

79 Anson Road, #06–04/06, Singapore 079906

Cambridge University Press is part of the University of Cambridge.

It furthers the University's mission by disseminating knowledge in the pursuit of education, learning and research at the highest international levels of excellence.

www.cambridge.org
Information on this title: www.cambridge.org/9781108438483 (Paperback)

© Cambridge Assessment International Education 2018

® IGCSE is a registered trademark

First published 2018

20 19 18 17 16 15 14 13 12 11 10 9 8 7 6 5

Printed in Great Britain by CPI Group (UK) Ltd, Croydon CR0 4YY

A catalogue record for this publication is available from the British Library

ISBN 978-1-108-43848-3 Paperback

Contents

Online lesson ideas for this book can be found at cambridge.org/9781108438483

Acknowledgements

The authors and publishers acknowledge the following sources of copyright material and are grateful for the permissions granted. While every effort has been made, it has not always been possible to identify the sources of all the material used, or to trace all copyright holders. If any omissions are brought to our notice, we will be happy to include the appropriate acknowledgements on reprinting.

Thanks to the following for permission to reproduce images:

Cover bgblue/Getty Images; Fig 4.1 FatCamera/E+/Getty images; Fig 5.2 Hero Images/Getty Images; Fig 6.2 concept map based on original by Marion Charreau www.territoiresdeslangues.com; Fig 9.2 Radius Images/Getty Images; Fig 9.3 DOMINIQUE FAGET/ AFP/Getty Images; Fig 9.4*t* Simona flamigni/istock/Getty Images; Fig 9.4 Jeffrey Greenberg/UIG/Getty Images; Fig 9.4*r* Ryan McVay/ Getty Images; Fig 10.1 Betsie Van Der Meer/Taxi/Getty Images; Fig 10.3 Cinderella388/istock/Getty Images; Fig 11.1 Tuayai/istock/ Getty Images; Fig 11.2 AzmanL/Getty Images; Fig 11.4 Fatih Erel/ Anadolu Agency/Getty Images; Fig 11.5 Betsie Van Der Meer/ The Image Bank/Getty Images; Lesson Idea 11.3 Photo 1 and Photo 2 © Paul Ellis

Introduction to the series by the editors

1

1 Approaches to learning and teaching Modern Foreign Languages

This series of books is the result of close collaboration between Cambridge University Press and Cambridge Assessment International Education, both departments of the University of Cambridge. The books are intended as a companion guide for teachers, to supplement your learning and provide you with extra resources for the lessons you are planning. Their focus is deliberately not syllabus-specific, although occasional reference has been made to programmes and qualifications. We want to invite you to set aside for a while assessment objectives and grading, and take the opportunity instead to look in more depth at how you teach your subject and how you motivate and engage with your students.

The themes presented in these books are informed by evidence-based research into what works to improve students' learning and pedagogical best practices. To ensure that these books are first and foremost practical resources, we have chosen not to include too many academic references, but we have provided some suggestions for further reading.

We have further enhanced the books by asking the authors to create accompanying lesson ideas. These are described in the text and can be found in a dedicated space online. We hope the books will become a dynamic and valid representation of what is happening now in learning and teaching in the context in which you work.

Our organisations also offer a wide range of professional development opportunities for teachers. These range from syllabus- and topic-specific workshops and large-scale conferences to suites of accredited qualifications for teachers and school leaders. Our aim is to provide you with valuable support, to build communities and networks, and to help you both enrich your own teaching methodology and evaluate its impact on your students.

Each of the books in this series follows a similar structure. In the third chapter, we have asked our authors to consider the essential elements of their subject, the main concepts that might be covered in a school curriculum, and why these are important. The next chapters give you a brief guide on how to interpret a syllabus or subject guide, and how to plan a programme of study. The authors will encourage you to think too about what is not contained in a syllabus and how you can pass on your own passion for the subject you teach.

The main body of the text takes you through those aspects of learning and teaching which are widely recognised as important. We would like to stress that there is no single recipe for excellent teaching, and that different schools, operating in different countries and cultures, will have strong traditions that should be respected. There is a growing consensus, however, about some important practices and approaches that need to be adopted if students are going to fulfil their potential and be prepared for modern life.

In the common introduction to each of these chapters, we look at what the research says and the benefits and challenges of particular approaches. Each author then focuses on how to translate theory into practice in the context of their subject, offering practical lesson ideas and teacher tips. These chapters are not mutually exclusive but can be read independently of each other and in whichever order suits you best. They form a coherent whole but are presented in such a way that you can dip into the book when and where it is most convenient for you to do so.

The final two chapters are common to all the books in this series and are not written by the subject authors. After the subject context chapters, we include guidance on how to reflect on your teaching and some avenues you might explore to develop your own professional learning. Schools and educational organisations are increasingly interested in the impact that classroom practice has on student outcomes. We have therefore included an exploration of this topic and some practical advice on how to evaluate the success of the learning opportunities you are providing for your students.

We hope you find these books accessible and useful. We have tried to make them conversational in tone so you feel we are sharing good practice rather than directing it. Above all, we hope that the books will inspire you and enable you to think in more depth about how you teach and how your students learn.

Paul Ellis and Lauren Harris

Series Editors

2 | Purpose and context

International research into educational effectiveness tells us that student achievement is influenced most by what teachers do in classrooms. In a world of rankings and league tables we tend to notice performance, not preparation, yet the product of education is more than just examinations and certification. Education is also about the formation of effective learning habits that are crucial for success within and beyond the taught curriculum.

The purpose of this series of books is to inspire you as a teacher to reflect on your practice, try new approaches and better understand how to help your students learn. We aim to help you develop your teaching so that your students are prepared for the next level of their education as well as life in the modern world.

This book will encourage you to examine the processes of learning and teaching, not just the outcomes. We will explore a variety of teaching strategies to enable you to select which is most appropriate for your students and the context in which you teach. When you are making your choice, involve your students: all the ideas presented in this book will work best if you engage your students, listen to what they have to say, and consistently evaluate their needs.

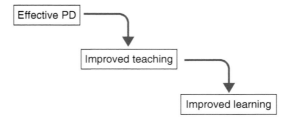

Cognitive psychologists, coaches and sports writers have noted how the aggregation of small changes can lead to success at the highest level. As teachers, we can help our students make marginal gains by guiding them in their learning, encouraging them to think and talk about how they are learning, and giving them the tools to monitor their success. If you take care of the learning, the performance will take care of itself.

When approaching an activity for the first time, or revisiting an area of learning, ask yourself if your students know how to:

- approach a new task and plan which strategies they will use
- monitor their progress and adapt their approach if necessary
- look back and reflect on how well they did and what they might do differently next time.

2 Approaches to learning and teaching Modern Foreign Languages

Effective students understand that learning is an active process. We need to challenge and stretch our students and enable them to interrogate, analyse and evaluate what they see and hear. Consider whether your students:

- challenge assumptions and ask questions
- try new ideas and take intellectual risks
- devise strategies to overcome any barriers to their learning that they encounter.

As we discuss in Chapter 6 **Active learning** and Chapter 8 **Metacognition**, it is our role as teachers to encourage these practices with our students so that they become established routines. We can help students review their own progress as well as getting a snapshot ourselves of how far they are progressing by using some of the methods we explore in Chapter 7 on **Assessment for Learning**.

Students often view the subject lessons they are attending as separate from each other, but they can gain a great deal if we encourage them to take a more holistic appreciation of what they are learning. This requires not only understanding how various concepts in a subject fit together, but also how to make connections between different areas of knowledge and how to transfer skills from one discipline to another. As our students successfully integrate disciplinary knowledge, they are better able to solve complex problems, generate new ideas and interpret the world around them.

In order for students to construct an understanding of the world and their significance in it, we need to lead students into thinking habitually about why a topic is important on a personal, local and global scale. Do they realise the implications of what they are learning and what they do with their knowledge and skills, not only for themselves but also for their neighbours and the wider world? To what extent can they recognise and express their own perspective as well as the perspectives of others? We will consider how to foster local and global awareness, as well as personal and social responsibility, in Chapter 11 on **Global thinking**.

As part of the learning process, some students will discover barriers to their learning: we need to recognise these and help students to overcome them. Even students who regularly meet success face their own challenges. We have all experienced barriers to our own learning at some point in our lives and should be able as teachers to empathise and share our own methods for dealing with these.

In Chapter 9 **Inclusive education** we discuss how to make learning accessible for everyone and how to ensure that all students receive the instruction and support they need to succeed as students.

Alongside a greater understanding of what works in education and why, we (as teachers) can also seek to improve how we teach and expand the tools we have at our disposal. For this reason, we have included Chapter 10 **Teaching with digital technologies**, discussing what this means for our classrooms and for us as teachers. Institutes of higher education and employers want to work with students who are effective communicators and who are information literate. Technology brings both advantages and challenges and we invite you to reflect on how to use it appropriately.

This book has been written to help you think harder about the impact of your teaching on your students' learning. It is up to you to set an example for your students and to provide them with opportunities to celebrate success, learn from failure and, ultimately, to succeed.

We hope you will share what you gain from this book with other teachers and that you will be inspired by the ideas that are presented here. We hope that you will encourage your school leaders to foster a positive environment that allows both you and your students to meet with success and to learn from mistakes when success is not immediate. We hope too that this book can help in the creation and continuation of a culture where learning and teaching are valued and through which we can discover together what works best for each and every one of our students.

3 | The nature of the subject

What are we talking about?

Modern Foreign Languages are three words that thrill. We're talking about something new, something exotic. We're talking code. We're talking mystery. We're trying to make sense of what we experience through different words. Modern Foreign Languages give us new windows onto the world, new tools, new ways of communicating, a new means of being us.

Modern Foreign Languages are evolving, flexible, something to play with. There are no boundaries to how much we can learn about them or how we can use them. We can create and innovate. We can invent phrases in contexts that have never previously existed. We can transform through speaking and writing how we see and describe what is around us.

In this book, we are going to talk with passion about Modern Foreign Languages and about how to develop that passion in our students. We are going to introduce you to ideas and approaches to help you confirm your love of languages, to reconnect with the subject you chose to teach, and to pass this onto the next generation.

What are we focusing on?

This book is about the learning and teaching of languages that are living and spoken today. It is about learning and teaching languages that are not native to your students and not normally used as the language of instruction. Depending on where you live, this might simply be any of the 6000-plus languages in the world!

We will be focusing on Modern Foreign Languages that are commonly taught in schools, but the approaches we will be looking at could also be applied to the teaching of other languages. The language you are teaching is most likely to be that of a nearby country or a language that is considered useful for commerce. Alternatively, it may be important for cultural or historic reasons.

We are not, however, looking at the teaching of English here. There's another book in this series specifically about that: *Approaches to Learning and Teaching English as a Second Language.*

Why study Modern Foreign Languages?

We've just given you a few ideas, but before we go any further, it is time for you to have a think. Take a moment or two to write down your initial reflections on each of these two questions:

1 *What inspired you to study another language?*
2 *What inspires your students to study another language?*

Did your answers to the first question differ much from your answers to the second question? If so, why do you think that was? Was your answer: 'Because they have to.'?

Now let's consider a third question:

3 *Why do some students not study another language?*

Did your answers to the third question make you think of other questions? How do you feel about students in your school who choose not to, or who are not allowed to, start or continue their study of another language? What reasons – good or bad – might there be?

Teacher Tip

Ask your colleagues and your students the same questions, especially when decisions are being made in your school about curriculum options or which examination subjects to take.

Many people choose to study another language because someone else inspired them to do so. A family member or friend may have encouraged them or, quite likely, it will have been their teacher. A colleague told me that the main reason he chose to study languages was because a teacher once provided constructive comments on an essay he wrote that were longer than the essay itself! The attitude of a teacher can make such a difference to the attitude of a student.

You can broaden your prospects of employment if you know another language. You might be able to work in another country or negotiate more easily with foreign business partners. When gaining qualifications that lead to eventual employment, you may want to study through another language or access materials only available in that language. This is often true of those with an interest in science, but it might also be, for example, a musicologist researching the context of a foreign composer.

Other people choose to study languages because it broadens their horizons. If you can communicate in another language, you can access a wider variety of materials and situations. This might be for leisure purposes to help with your basic needs when visiting a country where that language is spoken. It might be for cultural purposes so that you can, for example, read literature or understand lyrics in another language.

Some people choose to study another language simply because they discover they are good at it. Other people become linguists because it sets them apart, particularly in countries where few people continue their study of languages to a high level. Still others like the intellectual and cognitive challenge. There are also some people who seek to reinvent themselves and assume a different personality when communicating in another language.

Various studies suggest that learning languages is good for your brain and for your memory. It can boost your capacity to switch your attention fluently between projects and ideas; it can help you see new and different ways of doing things; and it can enable you to find nuances in what you or others are saying. It can make your brain more malleable and might even contribute to your chances of delaying the onset of dementia later in life.

If you consider any list of what are sometimes referred to as 21st-century skills, you will notice that linguists are particularly well disposed to ticking the vast majority of them. We are open-minded, collaborative and literate in a variety of ways. Linguists are also more likely to be tolerant and understanding, able to see other perspectives, and inclined to bring people together. Linguists usually have a positive attitude to other countries and cultures and are able to integrate.

What are we studying in Modern Foreign Languages?

At a basic level, the teaching of Modern Foreign Languages is about getting students to speak, read and write about many of the same things they can already talk about in their own language. We are providing students with the means of communicating, initially about quite simple, everyday things. For younger children, this can be fun and exciting and they will regularly go home to their parents and show off that they can count to ten or name their favourite animals in a different language.

Unless we keep them stimulated with new, meaningful activities, children may get frustrated by not being able to express all that they want to. However, this frustration doesn't usually manifest itself until they are considerably older. One of the reasons for this is that they are unlikely to understand how languages are constructed and learnt and the extent of their own language. They may also not appreciate the difference between active and passive skills (see Figure 3.1).

Depending on how a language is learnt, it is commonly either the passive skill of reading or the active skill of speaking that comes first. This will depend on the student's background and confidence. Reading often quickly overtakes other skills once we know a number of words and have a good understanding of grammar. If you have learnt other languages but not used them for a while, you will probably notice that your reading skills, if nothing else, have remained quite strong.

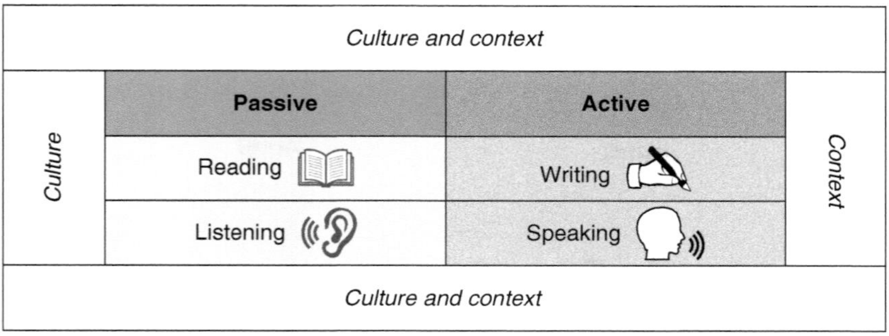

Figure 3.1: The four language skills.

Some students struggle when they are asked to listen to native speakers, whereas they often have less difficulty in understanding each other, probably because the accent and intonation have not yet been perfected. Give your students plenty of opportunity to familiarise themselves with the sounds of the foreign language, even if they understand very little at first. You could play an audio recording of a café or street scene in the background as students enter your room, for example.

Speaking and listening often go hand in hand – and are in fact sometimes examined together in formal assessments – as students are rarely asked to give monologues. They need the tools to be creative and we need to provide a safe and supportive environment in which they can take their initial steps. Some students think they sound silly and get embarrassed, whereas others are more than happy to have a go. We need to coach all students according to their strengths.

Writing is habitually the most difficult skill to master. This is because it is usually a solitary activity without immediate interaction. Some languages have more or less formalised ways of writing than students might be used to, or writing might be particularly challenging because students have to use a different alphabet or characters rather than words. A good teacher needs to balance the four skills while also situating them in the culture and context of the foreign language.

Teacher Tip

Spend time early on getting students to recognise the look and sound of the language you are teaching. Do so in a positive way, perhaps asking them to point out the similarities and differences to their own language.

Approaches to learning and teaching Modern Foreign Languages

When students are preparing for exams, consider their strengths in each of the four skills for each of the topics they are studying. As we will explore in the chapters that follow, techniques which some may consider old-fashioned are in fact very useful in cross-testing skills: dictations and vocabulary tests spring to mind. When reviewing topics regularly, check to what extent students are skilled both passively and actively in their use of the language.

Consider also whether they appreciate the meaning behind certain words and their cultural importance. For example, the word *boulangerie* in French translates as 'bakery', but this small shop that can be found in almost every village or district of a town or city also regularly plays a vital function in terms of community relations and even local gossip! Making reference in an essay or oral presentation to something that is particular to the language's culture shows great aptitude.

And don't forget that it is rare for a language only to be spoken in one country. Western European languages spread historically around the globe and it can be an interesting activity for students to research this, finding out where communities of speakers of certain languages have settled. Would they know, for example, that in Patagonia in Argentina, there are around 5000 Welsh speakers, or that the city of Melbourne in Australia has the largest Greek-speaking population outside Greece?

Teacher Tip

Displays in language classrooms are often some of the best you will see in schools. Keep up this tradition by filling your walls with maps and flags and plenty of interesting information about where languages are spoken and how cultures have mixed – or clashed!

Good textbooks these days explore where and how languages are used beyond their 'mother country'. Until quite recently, it was hard to obtain information about traditions and ways of life in certain countries. These days, it is considered normal for a teacher to have some knowledge of many places where a particular language is used.

Students enjoy finding out about exotic locations and it can be a boost to their interest in learning a language to realise that this may open up opportunities for them for work or travel. If you are struggling to convince your students that knowledge of another language can open up their world, ask them to do a project – in their own language if need be – about a country they would like to visit or the home country of a cultural or sporting icon. You may be surprised at just how much they engage in this task.

Summary

- You and your students will have multiple motivations for learning languages.

- There are many and sometimes surprising advantages of learning other languages.

- The study of languages involves passive and active skills: students are unlikely to be equally strong in each.

- It is important for students to appreciate the culture and context of languages.

- Students can be encouraged in their language learning by lively classroom displays and also by researching language connections through their other interests.

4 | Key considerations

Getting down to basics

What are the main building blocks of language learning? Is it important for students to use faultless grammar from the beginning or is it more important simply to get them communicating in the foreign language? If you have young children or come into contact with them, consider the errors they make as they explore their first language. To what extent should we compare their efforts with those of our students?

We will leave you to look at the research on first and second language acquisition; it is safe to say that there are both similarities and differences in the way we learn at these levels. As children, we don't think about the language we are learning – we soak it up from what is hopefully a stimulating and linguistically rich environment. For a while it was suggested that language teachers should try to recreate this in the classroom by exclusively using the 'target language', but this is often unrealistic.

If we look at some lessons from studies of bilingual education, we can quickly appreciate that there are different forms of communication. In essence, there is social language and there is academic language. And there is also classroom language somewhere between the two. If you work in a school with lots of international students, you may have noticed that some are very good at discussing everyday topics but are less fluent when vocabulary becomes more specific.

In terms of recreating a 'normal' environment of language immersion such as that experienced by young children, you may want to select which words and phrases should always be in the target language. Much vocabulary is repeated in lessons to the extent that it should become natural to hear and use it. Many teachers put up posters of classroom language as a memory aid, or insist students always greet them or ask for certain things from each other in the target language.

Teacher Tip

Make a list of common language that is used in your classroom. This might include phrases such as: *Open your books at page 15. / Sorry I'm late. / Can I borrow your pen? – Of course. Here you are.* Make sure students know how to pronounce the words. Make sure too that they will understand the response you will give them in the target language.

As we will see in Chapter 5 **Interpreting a syllabus**, vocabulary, grammar and structures need to be introduced in a systematic way and with purpose. At a very basic level, though, it is often more about letting students have a go, letting them talk about things they can relate to, and building their confidence. We can introduce new grammar subtly by encouraging students to look for patterns in the language and, in due course, affirming what they discover.

Back to the future

The learning of Modern Foreign Languages is a peculiar thing when you think about it. Students will often begin another language a decade or so after they first begin to speak – or if you are an adult, this will of course be many years later, but that's another story (and another book)! In effect, you are asking children to go back to the beginning and learn how to speak again, albeit using a different code. You are asking them to talk about things in a way that is initially quite regressive.

Interestingly, it can be the opposite when students reach a higher level. When studying for their IGCSE®s, students are already being challenged to consider topics they may never have spoken or written about in their own language. At pre-university level this is more evident, as they are asked to look at issues on which they may not yet have formed opinions. It can be difficult for students to debate or plan an essay about something political, ethical or otherwise controversial.

It is the same when we introduce foreign literature, history or other cultural aspects. To what extent have they already met such ideas in other parts of their curriculum? How much do they read in their own language? Do they have the necessary research skills? Have they developed cultural sensitivity? Just as it is important gradually to scaffold students' learning of vocabulary and grammar, you will need to spend time building up their appreciation of and approach to study at this level.

Teacher Tip

Share your programme of study with teachers of other subjects to encourage connections and consolidate learning. If you are planning on studying a historical period with your students, talk to the History department to see if they are also covering this period or have any advice. If you are going to be studying fiction, compare thoughts with literature specialists. If you are using statistics, don't forget the mathematicians either!

In some schools, certain subjects are taught through a foreign language. We have seen examples of this in History and Geography and also in Physical Education. This is usually done when a school has a particular focus on bilingual education or if a teacher of one of these subjects is fluent in another language. A part-bilingual curriculum needs careful management but can add an extra, valuable dimension to language learning.

The essentials

However enthusiastic we may be as teachers of Modern Foreign Languages, we have to accept that some of our students may not be quite as passionate about the subject as we are. In Chapter 3 **The nature of the subject**, we looked at some ways of encouraging students to opt in but we have to be realistic about how much some will want to achieve, with other demands and distractions on their minds. It is also worthwhile considering what fundamental aspects of foreign languages should be learnt by every student.

In his book *Future Wise*, David Perkins of Harvard Graduate School of Education makes the case for breaking down the school and individual subject curricula into learning that is likely to be useful for the life students might lead. He makes the distinction between 'understandings, questions and know-how' that are 'big' (for the many) and those that are 'niche' (for the few). It is quite easy to see how learning in some subjects is more specific than in others, but what about in ours?

Teacher Tip

Draw a table with columns labelled one, three, five and seven years. In each column, list the 'big understandings and know-how' you think students should obtain in these periods of time. Include which tenses students should be familiar with, what areas of vocabulary, and even the length or type of text students should be able to understand. For example, how important is it for all students to know all parts of a particular verb conjugation – are the first-person singular and plural enough? Is it essential for all students to understand the finer points of the subjunctive mood, or is this something only for those who want to specialise in languages?

You might want to share this with your students if you think they will find it motivating. In **Chapter 6 Active Learning** and **Chapter 8 Metacognition**, we'll look at how learning can best be constructed and retained.

At the lowest level, we would probably want our students to be able to recognise by sight and sound whichever language we are teaching, know where it is spoken and get a feel for the culture of those countries. This is the 'broadening of horizons' we mentioned in Chapter 3 **The nature of the subject**. We would also like our students, even after just a year of study, to have a passive understanding of quite a number of words and to be able to use some of them actively in the spoken or written form.

Inventing and asking students to practise role-plays is a good way of getting them to use the language both passively and actively. Many textbooks encourage conversations that lead to descriptions about students' family, house, or how many pets they have and what colour they are. These are fun, particularly for younger students, but how likely are students to use these words in the future? We are not suggesting you should avoid such role-plays, but where could or should we best focus?

Even students halfway through their degree have been known to struggle when faced with what should be everyday, useful conversations. They may be able to discuss environmental policy, but they may not be able to ask for a ticket at a railway station or understand directions given to them in the street. Surely one of our main goals as teachers of languages is to ensure those in our classes, however long they spend with us, feel confident in using the target language in real-life contexts?

Teacher Tip

To reflect more on this, think back to the last time you went to the country where the language you are teaching is spoken. What vocabulary and grammatical structures made a positive (or even vital!) difference to your stay, and which of these could easily be taught to and applied by your students?

At IGCSE level, there is a lot of scope for making students familiar with language they might come across later in their lives, even if they don't appreciate it at the time. For the language to stick, they need to see it as more than something to learn for an exam. Keep revisiting key phrases with them in your lessons, demonstrating in particular the basic structures that are common across several topic areas. If they practise enough, students should quickly be able to hold a reasonable conversation.

🖳 LESSON IDEA ONLINE 4.1: VOCABULARY IN A ROOM

A simple way to pick up new vocabulary quickly is to try to name everything in a room and then begin to link the words together. This lesson idea presents a way of doing this in a phased and manageable way.

To familiarise students of any age with the sound of the foreign language, introduce them to various forms of media. It is easy to find video or audio clips on the internet, including excerpts from film, television and radio. We will look at this in Chapter 10 **Teaching with digital technologies**. Students won't and don't need to understand every word, but exposure to the language as native speakers hear it will give them a sense of the sounds and cadences and make it feel more real.

Figure 4.1: Encourage students to watch and listen to the language they are learning using digital media.

4 Approaches to learning and teaching Modern Foreign Languages

You may be fortunate enough to have a language assistant in your school. This provides a great opportunity for your students to improve their oral skills at all ages and stages. You could guide the language assistant to focus on the topic you are teaching at the time, and this will be important when your students are preparing for high-stakes exams. But you may alternatively want to ask them to run a parallel curriculum, during which they simply concentrate on everyday conversation.

Depending on your proximity to a country where the language you are teaching is spoken, you may of course also have the possibility of spending some time there with students. If you do this, you will need to plan carefully, otherwise little language learning will take place. At pre-university level, many schools ask their students either to attend full-immersion language schools or carry out work experience. The latter is hard to organise, but can be extremely beneficial to language proficiency.

And last but not least: don't leave yourself out! New words and phrases are being added each year to the language you teach and you may have little opportunity to speak it with anyone other than your students. Set aside some time for yourself with your language assistant, if you have one, or fix a dedicated moment every day or week to read, write or think in the language you teach. It is essential to keep your own skills and love of language learning alive.

Summary

- The languages students need to communicate differs according to whether they are in a social or academic context.

- Many phrases are often repeated in class and so should always be in the target language.

- Give students plenty of practice in using and retaining common, everyday phrases.

- Language learning is about building vocabulary and grammar, but also about building cultural awareness and intellectual capability to discuss topics at a high level.

- Certain vocabulary and structures could be considered 'essential learning' for all, and others could be considered more 'niche', for students aiming to achieve an advanced level in the language.

Interpreting a syllabus

5

What is a curriculum?

Before we consider how to interpret a syllabus, let's go back at least one step and think about what a curriculum is. I was once asked this during an interview for a position that had the word in the job title and floundered not particularly intelligently but was somehow still appointed! It's not as straightforward as my online search engine tells me on the front page when I look up the word: 'the subjects comprising a course of study in a school or college'.

The word 'curriculum' is in fact used in several different ways. Some might interpret the word narrowly to refer to a prescribed range of courses for a particular school year group, or as a specific learning programme for a particular subject across a number of school years. Others might interpret it more broadly and holistically as the overall educational experience a student receives, including the subjects, their interconnections, how they are taught, and the school mission or ethos.

Schools choose their overall curriculum, encompassing all subjects and options for students, according to their context and values. Sometimes there are national requirements to adhere to and sometimes this is underpinned by the entry requirements for universities, if students choose to continue to higher education. Some schools choose to follow a curriculum prescribed fully by an international education organisation. Others allow greater flexibility and a wider mix.

All schools offer the study of languages somewhere in their curriculum. The first language of students or the language of study will certainly be available as an academic subject. It is not necessarily the case, however, that Modern Foreign Languages will feature. This may be because there is not enough space in the timetable, or that teachers are not available. Sometimes only some students are allowed to study foreign languages.

On occasion, teachers have to fight for the place of their subject in the school curriculum. Some governments might decide that a subject is 'too hard' for students to study beyond a certain age, or that it is not as relevant as others to a country's future prosperity. If you find yourself in this position, revise what we discussed in Chapter 3 **The nature of the subject**. As the Austrian philosopher Wittgenstein wrote in the 1920s, 'the limits of [your] language are the limits of [your] world.'

Teacher Tip

A useful exercise with post-16 students is to ask them to consider in depth the place of Modern Foreign Languages in the curriculum. You could prepare them to hold a 'hot-air balloon debate', asking each to represent a subject and vote at the end which subject should be thrown out to keep the hot-air balloon in the air. You might want to give extra help to the student representing foreign languages!

What is a syllabus?

Etymologically, the word *syllabus* derives from a modern Latin word for a list. (As a linguist, you'll want to know for sure what the plural should be: the good news is that, according to the Oxford English Dictionary, we can either say *syllabuses* or *syllabi*. The ending of the second of the alternatives mimics what might have been the plural had it been an ancient Latin word.) If we think of a syllabus as a list of items to cover, it becomes a convenient guide to what to teach.

A syllabus, then, is the contents page of an exciting language learning narrative you are going to weave for your students. As with the definition of a curriculum, this could mean what students will learn over one or several years of lessons. And as for a curriculum, this could be determined by national requirements, by your school, or by the manager of the faculty or department in which you work. Quite often, a syllabus document will have been written by another organisation.

When you are preparing students for external summative assessments, such as IGCSEs, A Levels, the IB Diploma, or Advanced Placement, you will have access to a syllabus (also known as a subject guide) compiled by whichever organisation will be assessing your students' work. In effect, this document is a contract between them and the student, with you as the interpreter. It is essential that you get to know this document well, and explain it to your students so that they understand what is required of them.

5 Approaches to learning and teaching Modern Foreign Languages

For whatever reason, you may not have a choice of syllabus. If you do, how should you choose? At IGCSE level in Modern Foreign Languages, there isn't a huge amount of variety between the topics and grammar available for study. There can be quite considerable differences in what is on offer post-16, however, and it is important to compare syllabuses. The students will still study the four language skills (as shown in Figure 3.1) but the topics available for in-depth study (e.g. literature, culture) vary a lot.

When choosing topics for older students, think again of your school's context and values. Think also of what is likely to be most engaging for your students because of their interests or because of the interests you would like to cultivate in them. Think too, of course, of yourself as their teacher. There is little point in choosing topics that you know little about or for which you hold little interest. You need to be able to encourage your students through your own motivation!

Teacher Tip

Take a moment to reflect on what your ideal syllabus for advanced level (pre-university) students would contain. Which aspects of society and which aspects of culture would you like to cover? How closely does this resemble what you are teaching? How can you make your course more inviting and exciting?

All exam syllabus documents contain certain features that should be clearly set out. These will normally include:

- a brief description of the assessing organisation that has designed the syllabus
- a clear statement of the aims and topics of the syllabus
- a clear statement of what is being assessed and how
- an indication of how many 'guided learning hours' (contact time) students should be expected to spend with their teacher to do well in the course
- the support available for the teacher in terms of resources and training.

The syllabus document will then give a detailed description of each of the components. For Modern Foreign Languages courses at IGCSE level, there will usually be examinations on each of the four skills: Reading, Writing, Speaking and Listening, although the last two may sometimes be combined because some schools do not have the facilities to administer listening tests. At pre-university level, students may also be assessed, often through writing, on their in-depth knowledge of a topic.

It is your duty as a teacher to prepare students to do the best they can in their summative assessments in terms of ensuring that they fulfil the syllabus requirements and that deadlines are not missed. If you are teaching within a wider school programme, there may be a curriculum coordinator in your school who also keeps an eye on such things, but your students are placing their trust in you to get it right. For this reason as well, make sure you are using the right syllabus!

It is important, therefore, that you keep up-to-date with any changes in the syllabus. Some such documents don't change very often but others have minor alterations made to them every year. Look out for vertical lines in the margin next to certain words or paragraphs as these normally indicate that something has recently changed and you should take note of it. The latest version of the syllabus document should be available on the examining organisation's website.

How to start planning

Fortunately, not all teaching is about preparation for exams. Particularly in the lower years, when students are beginning to discover the joy of learning languages, you have greater flexibility in what to do with your students and in what order. This said, you cannot of course do whatever you like! Unless you are the only teacher of Modern Foreign Languages in your school, you have to design in collaboration with other teachers a cohesive programme of study.

To avoid confusion and for the ease of simplicity, from now on we use the following terms with these meanings:

- **Curriculum:** the whole-school approach to the teaching and learning of the target language
- **Syllabus:** a document to guide you on how to prepare students for a specific milestone (often an examination)
- **Programme of study:** the knowledge and language skills your students will have acquired by the end of a particular period of time.

5

Approaches to learning and teaching Modern Foreign Languages

The programme of study is normally written by and for teachers in the school and designed to ensure that students learn similar things even if they are in different classes with different teachers. It sets out the language and topics to be learnt and in which order, in order to achieve the 'objectives' and the expected (or hoped for) 'outcomes' listed in the syllabus. It is the document you will refer to most regularly, but remember it is set within the context of the syllabus and curriculum (see Figure 5.1 below).

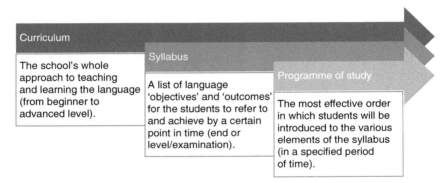

Figure 5.1

'Objectives' are the aims for students of individual sections of the programme, such as *to learn how to describe where you live*. 'Outcomes' give greater detail about the language and skills students would be expected to show if the 'objectives' are fulfilled. These might include a set of regularly used words to talk or write about your house or city, or adjectives and knowledge about how they must 'agree' with nouns. They might also include the ability to hold a conversation or write a short essay.

There may be grammar or vocabulary that students are expected to master before they can continue their study to the next level. They may also have to attain a certain grade in summative tests before they are allowed by their school to pursue languages as a subject. A programme of study must therefore also be considered as a step to the next stage. It must be designed inclusively so that students can bridge the gap to and access the next level.

As we will see in Chapter 6 **Active learning**, you need to help students construct their knowledge and find ways of retaining it. A teacher cannot just lecture from the front or read from a textbook and expect a miraculous transfer to the brains of their students. You must therefore plan your programme of study carefully so that students gradually build up their knowledge of the language you are teaching and you must provide scaffolding that you only remove once students are confident and ready.

Teacher Tip

Think of a basic part of grammar in the language you teach. What are the stages students would need to go through before mastering it? Think of every tiny step along the way, including where there might be exceptions. Compare this in your mind to a construction worker building a house. What needs to come first? What needs to be secured before the next piece?

The textbooks we mentioned a moment ago can be a big help in planning the order in which you should teach the language. Don't become over-reliant on this, though, or your lessons might become tedious or irrelevant. Part of the joy of being a teacher is creating new approaches to learning – one of the objectives of this book is to help you do just that. The key thing is to know what needs to be covered in your programme of study and when.

One last but vital comment about how to plan what you teach before we move on is about training and professional development. All reputable educational organisations offer opportunities for you to attend courses run by experts in the subject or syllabus you are teaching. Some exam providers make such training compulsory. It is in your interests to attend training on a regular basis, both to answer your questions and to share thoughts and resources with other teachers.

Create regular opportunities as well to talk to colleagues in your school who are teaching the same or other languages. One colleague may be an expert on an aspect of the syllabus or on using certain resources or tools. Find the time to discuss how you teach languages and to observe each other in action. Invite a 'critical friend' to sit at the back of your classroom and make notes on one aspect of your teaching, for example how you give feedback – and do the same for them.

Figure 5.2: Reflecting on your lesson with a critical friend.

Beyond the syllabus

In preparation for this book, we looked at a range of pre-university level exam syllabuses and our first reaction was that the topics have changed very little since we were at school. As a teacher, it's hard yet again to talk about politics with apathetic teenagers or health issues with embarrassed adolescents. You often have little or no choice in a restrictive syllabus, but you can still engage your students' interest in a positive way.

Even if you are preparing students for an examination, don't forget what brought you and them to the subject in the first place: a love of learning languages. It is too easy to get tied up in the demands of a syllabus, its aims and assessments, and suddenly to realise when it's too late that the passion you shared for language learning has gone. Be sure to inject some enthusiasm into your language classroom from time to time! In Chapter 11 **Global thinking**, we'll look in more detail about how to do this.

Teacher Tip

Select a topic from a pre-university level exam syllabus and write it in the centre of a large piece of paper. Now draw a mind map (or spider chart), preferably using the language you teach, to brainstorm all the mini-topics you could cover. Now rate each of these according to how interesting and/or useful they are likely to be for your students (remember the 'big understandings, questions and know-how' we mentioned in Chapter 4 **Key considerations**). Don't bore yourself or them with aspects of the topic that are tedious, but seek to challenge and extend them too.

It's worth taking students of any age beyond the prescribed syllabus and into an exploration of the people who speak the language you are teaching. Tell them about shared histories, uniqueness and cultural quirks. Invite them to research and do projects on aspects that appeal to them. Get them to appreciate that the language you are teaching is alive outside your classroom. Set the language in context and give your students lots of opportunities to use it confidently and effectively.

LESSON IDEA 5.1: CHANGING THE WORDS

Students love doing absurd things with language, and it's a good way to help them remember it. When they have understood enough of the basics of a particular grammatical point, such as the equivalent in the language you are teaching of *She ate the chocolate in the park with her friends*, invite them gradually to change one word at a time until the sentence becomes completely different. Your students will soon be using the language creatively and competitively!

You might want to think of your whole programme of study for your language as a large jigsaw. (If you are artistic, or know someone who is, you could create a display for your classroom.) Imagine each piece of the jigsaw as a topic such as *my family*, *my house*, *my city*, and post lists of common words to describe each. With enough grammar and phrases, students should eventually be able to speak in some detail about themselves using the entire jigsaw as a visual reminder.

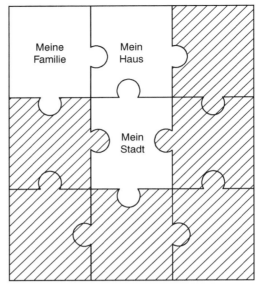

Figure 5.3: Piecing together a topic.

There are many ways of interpreting a syllabus. Above all, be clear about what you are teaching and make this as clear and open as possible to your students as well. Ensure they are happy with why they are studying languages and that they know what they are going to cover in your lessons. Recap, review and revise, and provide plenty of creative opportunities to use the language you are teaching to keep students motivated in their learning.

Summary

- The values of the school and the community and country where you are teaching may determine the overall curriculum and, consequently, your teaching.

- Regardless of the curriculum or syllabus, there are always opportunities to make language learning an engaging and creative experience.

- Use your lesson planning to adapt or supplement the syllabus so that your students' language learning journey is interesting and challenging.

- Seek regular opportunities to continue your own professional development and improve your teaching skills and your understanding of the syllabus you are teaching.

Active learning

6

What is active learning?

Active learning is a pedagogical practice that places student learning at its centre. It focuses on *how* students learn, not just on *what* they learn. We as teachers need to encourage students to 'think hard', rather than passively receive information. Active learning encourages students to take responsibility for their learning and supports them in becoming independent and confident learners in school and beyond.

Research shows us that it is not possible to transmit understanding to students by simply telling them what they need to know. Instead, we need to make sure that we challenge students' thinking and support them in building their own understanding. Active learning encourages more complex thought processes, such as evaluating, analysing and synthesising, which foster a greater number of neural connections in the brain. While some students may be able to create their own meaning from information received passively, others will not. Active learning enables all students to build knowledge and understanding in response to the opportunities we provide.

Why adopt an active learning approach?

We can enrich all areas of the curriculum, at all stages, by embedding an active learning approach.

In active learning, we need to think not only about the content but also about the process. It gives students greater involvement and control over their learning. This encourages all students to stay focused on their learning, which will often give them greater enthusiasm for their studies. Active learning is intellectually stimulating and taking this approach encourages a level of academic discussion with our students that we, as teachers, can also enjoy. Healthy discussion means that students are engaging with us as a partner in their learning.

Students will better be able to revise for examinations in the sense that revision really is 're-vision' of the ideas that they already understand.

Active learning develops students' analytical skills, supporting them to be better problem solvers and more effective in their application of knowledge. They will be prepared to deal with challenging and unexpected situations. As a result, students are more confident in continuing to learn once they have left school and are better equipped for the transition to higher education and the workplace.

What are the challenges of incorporating active learning?

When people start thinking about putting active learning into practice, they often make the mistake of thinking more about the activity they want to design than about the learning. The most important thing is to put the student and the learning at the centre of our planning. A task can be quite simple but still get the student to think critically and independently. Sometimes a complicated task does not actually help to develop the student's thinking or understanding at all. We need to consider carefully what we want our students to learn or understand and then shape the task to activate this learning.

Facilitating active learning in language lessons

Educator and philosopher John Dewey said: 'Give the pupils something to do, not something to [rote] learn, and if the doing is of such a nature as to demand thinking, learning naturally results.' As language teachers, our role is to encourage this thinking, ensuring that students are engaging with the target language and using their new linguistic knowledge and skills to express themselves.

Ultimately, we want students to take ownership of their learning and become autonomous in as many aspects of their language journey as possible.

The active language classroom has implications for the role of the teacher as well as the role and expectations of students. A focus on active learning encourages a shift from teacher–centred to student–centred activities and a shift from product-driven to process–driven learning. This means we should always be thinking about how learning is taking place, not just focusing on the end result of that learning. It doesn't mean, however, that we are doing any less. It means that we are there to guide our students through carefully planned activities that are designed to offer opportunities to collaborate, build on knowledge and skills, and, most importantly, develop their abilities to think and make reasoned judgements about the language they are using and why.

Table 6.1 below compares the role played by teachers and learners in a teacher-centred and learner-centred classroom.

The role of the teacher	
Teacher-centred classroom	**Learner-centred classroom**
Focus on the product of learning	Focus on the process of learning
Teacher as transmitter of knowledge	Teacher as organiser of knowledge
Teacher as 'doer' for students	Teacher as 'enabler' facilitating learning
Subject-specific focus	Holistic learning focus

The role of the learner	
Teacher-centred classroom	**Learner-centred classroom**
Passive recipients of knowledge	Active participants taking responsibility for their own learning
Focused on answering questions	Asking questions
Competing with one another	Collaborating in their learning
Learners of individual subjects	Connecting their learning

Table 6.1
Source: *Active Learning and Teaching Methods for Key Stage 3*, Northern Ireland.

Fostering independent learners

Students often feel constrained by what they feel they can (or rather, can't) say. We need to make sure that students are not confined to what we as teachers can provide, but also give them the skills and the tools they need to be able to discover and experiment with new language for themselves. This might include making verb tables and dictionaries available and ensuring students know how to use them, or spending some time exploring different online translation tools and discussion forums. We need to encourage students to critically evaluate the reliability of the various online tools they use.

Outside the classroom there is ample opportunity for students to explore their own areas of interest. This might be listening to French rap, reading a fashion blog in Italian, accessing the news in German or watching a TV series in Portuguese. It's important that our students are taking every opportunity possible to practise outside the classroom. Encourage them to find cheap and practical ways of practising the language. For example, they can record themselves speaking using their phones or they could even practise talking to themselves in the target language in their heads!

Teacher Tip

Encourage your students to share links to interesting things they find in the target language, for example, blogs, videos or magazines. You could set up a shared online learning space to encourage this.

Questioning

By using a range of questions in our language lessons we can help develop students' thinking skills and encourage them to build on what they already know and are able to do. Many teachers use the cognitive dimension of Bloom's revised taxonomy, which works from lower-order thinking skills (remembering, understanding, applying) through to higher-order thinking skills (analysing, evaluating and creating) to help them to ask better questions.

As language teachers, we often ask questions at the lower-order thinking end of the scale to determine whether students remember key vocabulary, understand conjugations and can apply a particular grammar rule for example. This is because the language required for some of the higher-order thinking activities is often more advanced. However, we can still challenge our students' thinking skills and check their understanding by asking questions that are *about* the target language as well as *in* the target language.

Look at the example questions in Figure 6.1 and think about how you could adapt them for a topic you are teaching.

The final stage in Bloom's, 'create', is too frequently neglected. However, manipulating the language we have learned to create something new is often very satisfying. Create opportunities for students to demonstrate their abilities as linguists by allowing them to build on their knowledge to produce something of their own.

	Thinking skill	Example questions
Higher order	**Creating** Combining ideas to make something new	Which words that we've used before will be useful in our presentation? Can you write a new ending to this story?
	Evaluating Discriminating between ideas and making judgements based on reasoned argument	Which of these paragraphs is the most effective? Why? If you could look up one word in the dictionary to help you to understand this text, which word will you choose and why?
	Analysing Breaking down information, identifying patterns, exploring relationships and solving problems	What pattern can you see in these endings? If 'a + el = al' in Spanish, what do you think will happen to 'de + el'? Here are some nouns we've never met before. Can you work out what they might mean? Who do you think the author wrote this text for?
Lower order	**Applying** Applying knowledge or understanding in new contexts	If this verb looks like this when it follows 'on', what would you expect these verbs to look like when they follow 'on'? What would happen if you put 'no' before the verb in this sentence?
	Understanding Making sense of ideas	What did we learn last lesson about how possessive pronouns work? Can you give me an example of a verb that takes the present tense of 'être' to form the perfect tense?
	Remembering Recalling information	Which comparison structures did we learn last lesson? Which words in this sentence do you already know?

Figure 6.1: *Bloom's Revised Taxonomy* (L.W. Anderson and D.R. Krathwohl, 2001).

As well as asking questions about the target language that build students' metalinguistic skills, think about how you can also increase the challenge and extend students' thinking in the target language. When students are answering Reading or Listening comprehension questions for example, encourage them to build on their answers and promote discussion: *Pourquoi?* (Why?) *Kannst du mir ein weiteres Beispiel nennen?* (Can you give me another example?)

Planning for questions and activities in schemes of work and in individual lesson plans is a key way to ensure sufficient challenge in your language lessons.

Teacher Tip

When setting homework, encourage students to record any questions about areas they weren't sure about so that they can ask a classmate, or you, in the next lesson.

Who asks the questions?

We need to ensure that students aren't simply expected to answer the questions we pose, but to ask questions themselves. We need to encourage students to self-question, to question each other and to feel comfortable asking us, their teachers, questions. Make sure that you give students the necessary question words and the sentence stems in the target language early in their studies. Display these on the walls around the classroom as visual prompts. This offers support when they want to check the language in a question we are posing, as well as providing them with the language they will need to ask their own questions.

Questions that students ask shouldn't be limited to checking whether something is correct. Encourage students to ask questions that promote discussion about a topic or a strategy they are using or to question why language is behaving in a particular way – and give them the language to be able to do this!

LESSON IDEA 6.1: ROLE-PLAY

This role-play activity can be practised in groups or as a whole class and gives students plenty of opportunity to practise asking questions. Assign one student a particular role and put them in the 'hot seat' (for example, this role could be their favourite football player if you are discussing employment). The rest of their group, or the whole class, asks the person in the 'hot seat' questions about their life. It can also be a useful exercise for practising topic-specific vocabulary or particular tenses, depending on the characters and situation you create.

Setting the right task

If you want students to think and engage with their learning, you need to set them tasks that require them to do this. Bloom's taxonomy provides a useful framework to check where on the scale from lower- to higher-order thinking skills you are expecting your students to engage with the task you have set them.

Look at the activities in the list and decide where you would place them on Bloom's taxonomy:

- Listen to these people talking and say whether the following sentences are true or false.
- Read this text and decide which grade it is and why.
- Use this text and adapt it to talk about your own free time.
- Read the text and find all the activities.
- Use the article you have just read and the ten new words you have identified to create your own text.
- Arrange the texts you have been given according to their grammatical complexity.

Concept mapping

A useful task that encourages students to engage on a deeper level is creating their own concept maps. A concept map is a tool that helps students organise and represent their knowledge and understanding of a particular idea. The process of creating a concept map allows students to

Approaches to learning and teaching Modern Foreign Languages

structure their thoughts, make connections between ideas and work out where they are in relation to their learning objectives. The main idea, or concept, appears in the centre of the map with connected concepts stemming from it. Concept maps can be used to support vocabulary learning by connecting words or concepts with definitions, examples, synonyms and antonyms or might be used to organise ideas and language needed for a written piece of work.

As students learn new information, encourage them to reflect on their concept maps and make decisions about how what they already know relates to new material. Students can then add to, or modify, their maps.

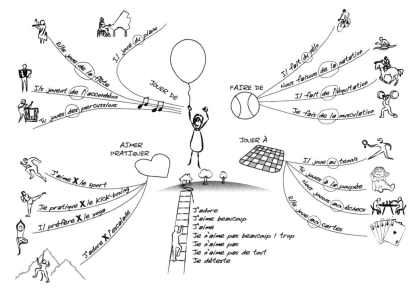

Figure 6.2: Concept map.

Teacher Tip

Before asking students to create individual concept maps, why not create a group concept map, or even one for the class? Ask students to think about what they already know about a topic and write any key words and related concepts on sticky notes. You will probably find that students' ideas will reflect different associations and categorisations. Ask students to work together to organise their ideas – sticky notes are helpful as students can re-organise information into new categories and subcategories as they negotiate among themselves. Once you have modelled this process with the class, students will find it easier to create their own concept maps for different topics in the future.

Collaborative learning

It can be much more effective for students to build ideas together rather than forming ideas alone. Students feel responsible for their learning and also an obligation to each other. In addition, if students know that their product, or a group product, is going to be more widely viewed by the rest of the class or exchanged with another class, they may be more motivated to engage.

> ☑ **LESSON IDEA ONLINE 6.2: RUNNING DICTATION**
> Lesson idea 6.2 gives students the opportunity to practise their four skills (as shown in Figure 3.1), reflect on their learning strategies and introduces some healthy competition!

When students learn collaboratively, it allows for discussion, peer feedback, reflection and improvement. It can also encourage students to develop a more creative approach to their own learning, through interaction, exchange of ideas and wider use of the target language. When students produce work collaboratively, they are more likely to make judgements about their learning throughout the process, instead of producing a finished piece of work and relying on teacher feedback at the end in order to improve their work. This means that feedback becomes part of the process of learning. Here are three suggestions on how to get students working collaboratively:

1 Jigsaw reading activities are popular in textbooks and frequently appear in language classrooms. Organise students into groups of three. Give each student a different section of an article to read (one student the beginning, one student the middle and a third student the end of the article). Tell students that they cannot show each other their section of the article but must work together to answer a series of questions about the article. Students need to talk to each other in

order to complete the task so they will be practising their speaking skills. You can do a similar activity to practise listening skills where each student listens to different information (perhaps different people being interviewed about the same topic).

2 Speed debating is useful for enabling students to practise and rehearse new vocabulary, sentence structures and ideas and allows for peer scaffolding. Set up the chairs in your classroom in two concentric circles. The students sitting in the outer circle face inwards and the students in the inner circle face outwards so students are facing each other. Pose a question or a statement that you want students to discuss and give them 1–2 minutes to do this with their partner. When the time is up, ask the outer circle to move one place to the left and the inner circle to remain seated so that everyone has a new partner. The process of exchanging opinions or information begins again. This can be repeated as many times as you feel is useful.

3 Progressive mind mapping is useful in encouraging students to share what they know and to demonstrate understanding. Divide the class into small groups and give each group a large piece of paper and a different coloured pen. Ask students to record a specific question or topic on which you want them to focus in the middle of the page. Give the groups 5–10 minutes to brainstorm ideas (words, concepts, etc. depending on the question). When the time has finished, ask the groups to keep their coloured pens and rotate so they are with another group's piece of paper. Then give them a further 5–10 minutes to add things that may be missing or to provide more detail. This can continue until they arrive back at their original piece of paper. Now ask the group to review what others have added, decide what they agree and disagree with, and what they are going to change and why.

Managing collaborative learning

Think about where your students sit more generally in your lessons. Sitting next to the same person all year might encourage the same thinking time and time again. Get the students to move around and work with different people. In an increasingly connected world, they may be required to work remotely with people from all over the world and move from one team to another frequently.

To ensure that group work is effective, we need to manage it carefully. Ensure that when students work together in a group, everyone has a role and that they collectively take responsibility for their group's success in completing the task. Depending on the activity, these roles can be rotated to ensure that everyone has the chance to practise the different skills.

LESSON IDEA ONLINE 6.3: COLLABORATIVE WRITING
Lesson idea 6.3 will give students the opportunity to practise their listening and writing skills while working collaboratively.

Provide clear and explicit instructions in the target language. It is helpful to recycle phrases when giving instructions so that students become familiar with them. Give students the instructions in a number of ways to reinforce them. This might be verbally, by demonstrating what you want them to do as well as writing them on the board.

It's important that something happens as a result of the language being produced by students and we need to make this outcome explicit to our students. For example, this might be solving a problem or gaining new information.

Summary

- Encourage students to take responsibility for their own learning, to ask questions, and to think.

- Equip students with the necessary skills to continue their language learning once they leave the classroom.

- Ask a range of questions that draw on higher-order thinking skills as well as lower-order thinking skills to challenge and extend students' thinking.

- Group work needs to be carefully set up and managed. Everyone needs to play a part and there should be a clear outcome for the group.

7 Assessment for Learning

What is Assessment for Learning?

Assessment for Learning (AfL) is a teaching approach that generates feedback that can be used to improve students' performance. Students become more involved in the learning process and, from this, gain confidence in what they are expected to learn and to what standard. We as teachers gain insights into a student's level of understanding of a particular concept or topic, which helps to inform how we support their progression.

We need to understand the meaning and method of giving purposeful feedback to optimise learning. Feedback can be informal, such as oral comments to help students think through problems, or formal, such as the use of rubrics to help clarify and scaffold learning and assessment objectives.

Why use Assessment for Learning?

By following well-designed approaches to AfL, we can understand better how our students are learning and use this to plan what we will do next with a class or individual students (see Figure 7.1). We can help our students to see what they are aiming for and to understand what they need to do to get there. AfL makes learning visible; it helps students understand more accurately the nature of the material they are learning and understand themselves as learners. The quality of interactions and feedback between students and teachers becomes critical to the learning process.

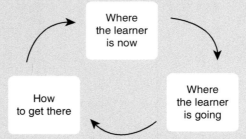

Figure 7.1: How can we use this plan to help our students?

We can use AfL to help our students focus on specific elements of their learning and to take greater responsibility for how they might move forward. AfL creates a valuable connection between assessment and learning activities, as the clarification of objectives will have a direct impact on how we devise teaching and learning strategies. AfL techniques can support students in becoming more confident in what they are learning, reflective in how they are learning, more likely to try out new approaches, and more engaged in what they are being asked to learn.

What are the challenges of incorporating AfL?

The use of AfL does not mean that we need to test students more frequently. It would be easy to just increase the amount of summative assessment and use this formatively as a regular method of helping us decide what to do next in our teaching. We can judge how much learning has taken place through ways other than testing, including, above all, communicating with our students in a variety of ways and getting to know them better as individuals.

Establishing what students already know

Before we think about what we want our students to do next, it's important to be clear about what they already know and understand. We need to consider what students need to know in order to access the next step and make sure we have checked any gaps in understanding or misconceptions before continuing.

Teacher Tip

Reflect on your previous lesson and write down the key ideas that you assume students now know and understand. Think of a quick activity that you can use to check this in the first 5 minutes of your next lesson. Lesson idea 7.1 suggests some that you may like to try.

LESSON IDEA 7.1: TRUE / FALSE STATEMENTS / WIPE-OUT / CARD SORT

True/False statements: Based on common misconceptions, devise statements about when to use the 'perfetto' and when to use the 'imperfetto' in Italian, for example. Students must then decide which are true and which are false and be able to explain why they have made their decision.

Wipe-out: Devise a short list of questions that will help you determine the level of comprehension for key concepts amongst your students. Ask students to record their answers on mini whiteboards or simply in their notebooks and hold their answers up. This allows you to quickly gauge the level of understanding for concepts that you have just taught, as well as activate prior knowledge for your students before moving on. For example, you might ask students: *Which Spanish verb 'to be' do we use to describe someone's appearance, 'ser' or 'estar'?*

Card sort: This activity gives students the opportunity to work with vocabulary, terms and concepts. Ask your students to sort the cards into meaningful pairs or categories. Sorting the cards gives students a structure to discuss content with one another and helps teachers check for understanding. Discuss with students what they have decided and ask them to explain why they sorted their cards into particular categories. For example, you might provide students with a set of cards where each card has a different verb on it. Students might sort the cards into three categories: *er*, *re* and *ir* verbs or perhaps they will sort them into two categories: verbs that take *avoir* in the perfect tense and verbs that take *être* in the perfect tense.

Setting clear targets for learning

The first step in successful AfL is for us to be clear about what we would like our students to achieve in a particular activity or lesson. For many teachers, this takes the form of a **learning goal** and set of **success criteria**. A learning goal identifies what we want our students to learn and the success criteria illustrate how students will demonstrate what they have learned. Learning goals and success criteria encourage students to take responsibility for their own learning because they understand what they are going to learn and how they will know whether they have succeeded. When sharing learning goals with students also explain the reason you would like them to learn something – students are more motivated when they can see the purpose.

In order to create suitable learning goals and accompanying success criteria, it is useful to ask yourself the following questions:

- What do I want my students to know, understand and be able to do?
- How will I know that learning has taken place?
- What does success look like?

Let's look at an example. In a French lesson focusing on verbs, a teacher might record the learning goal and success criteria on the board as in Figure 7.2.

Today I will:
- learn about verbs
- practise using 'er' verbs.

I can:
- explain to my classmate what a verb is
- recognise an 'er' verb
- find the stem of an 'er' verb
- use the correct ending of an 'er' verb for each subject person.

Figure 7.2: An example of a learning goal and success criteria.

Teacher Tip

Use clear, simple and student-friendly language when sharing learning goals.

It's helpful to think about the knowledge we want our students to acquire as well as the skill they will use in applying the knowledge. Here you can see that we want students to know what a verb is and then to be able to use '*er*' verbs successfully in context.

It is also important that we make the knowledge and skills explicit without limiting these to a specific context. For example, we could have written: *Today I will practise using 'er' verbs to talk about everyday activities*. However, by decontextualising the learning goal we ensure that the focus is on the process of the skill, which should be understood as transferable to future learning, regardless of the topic.

The 'I can' statements provide the success criteria. They offer a useful breakdown of the learning goal and a framework for students and teachers to use in order to check whether students can demonstrate what they have learned and where further help may be needed.

Refer to the learning goal and the success criteria during the lesson – not just at the end and allow time at the beginning for your students to discuss and perhaps negotiate the success criteria.

Teacher Tip

Think about whether you can use success criteria that begin with *I can explain to my classmate ...* . If your students can explain something clearly to someone else it suggests that they have understood and helps reinforce their own learning.

Helping students to recognise what success looks like

If students have played a role in identifying the success criteria for a particular learning goal, they are more likely to take ownership of their progress and internalise the criteria. There are a number of ways in which teachers can work together with students to co-construct criteria in language lessons. Here are some ideas to get started.

LESSON IDEA 7.2: CO-CONSTRUCTING CRITERIA

Jigsaw writing: Cut an example email into several pieces. In pairs, ask students to reassemble the email. To do this, students have to engage with the content of the email and analyse the various elements. It also provides them with a model that exemplifies what they are aiming for. For example, they might identify elements such as including an appropriate ending and closing and/or describing events using the relevant tense and offering opinions.

Producing an article: Share with your students three excellent examples of articles produced by students in another class. Then ask them to highlight the features that make them successful. It is helpful if you guide them by asking them to focus on specific features. This might be vocabulary, use of connectives, particular grammatical features or a narrative formula, such as information + opinion + reason + example. You might also want to show students an excellent example alongside a less successful example. This comparative exercise can be effective in highlighting how improvements can be made.

Eliciting evidence of understanding

We have established what our students already know. We have shared or constructed together the learning goals and success criteria for the lesson, and we feel confident that students understand 'what good looks like'. It is now up to us to ensure that we design effective classroom discussions and activities that will elicit evidence of learning. This enables us to determine where our students are in relation to the goal we have set and provide them with feedback to progress their learning. Here are some ideas to encourage discussion amongst your students and to help generate evidence of learning.

Asking the right questions

By asking the right questions we can challenge our students' thinking and encourage them to build on their ideas. Well-crafted questions also enable us to get to the heart of what our students have understood and where the gaps remain. It's important that we interpret students' answers rather than just evaluating them.

Hinge questions

There are often important concepts in a lesson that it is crucial our students understand before they move on. This might be understanding the difference between *por* and *para* in Spanish or the German case system, for example. These are sometimes referred to as 'hinge points'. A well-designed question can help us to check understanding of a particular concept and help us decide whether we can move on or whether a concept needs revisiting. An effective hinge question should be:

- quick for students to answer
- easy for teachers to assess all students' answers (e.g. multiple choice)
- hard to answer correctly if the student hasn't fully understood
- based around common misconceptions.

In a Spanish lesson, an example of a hinge question could be:

Which of the following sentences is the correct translation for 'I give the pen to him'?

A.	*Yo lo doy el bolígrafo.*	Pronoun error
B.	*Yo doy le el bolígrafo.*	Pronoun placement error
C.	*Yo le doy el bolígrafo.*	Correct answer
D.	*Yo doy lo el bolígrafo.*	Pronoun and pronoun placement error
E.	*Yo doy el bolígrafo le.*	Pronoun placement error
F.	*Yo doy el bolígrafo lo.*	Pronoun and pronoun placement error

Figure 7.3

This question is effective because it has been based on two common difficulties: which pronoun to choose and where in a sentence the pronoun should appear. If students select an incorrect answer it should help you to identify what they are having trouble with: is it pronoun selection, pronoun placement or both?

Hinge questions need responses from the whole class. You could elicit answers to this question by asking students to write their answers in their books and hold them up or by using cards which students hold up to show which sentence (A–F) they think is correct.

Teachers who use questioning techniques effectively often ask follow-up questions to extend and challenge their students' thinking and learning. Ask students why they have given a particular response or if they can think of another example.

Teacher Tip

When you plan your lesson, prepare exactly which questions you are going to ask and include them in your planning. Think carefully about how you word the questions to ensure they are pitched at the right level for your students. Share your questions with colleagues. Don't just discuss the question itself but how it worked in practice – it's the interactions provoked by the question that provide the useful information.

Asking the right questions in the right way

Wait time

When you ask your students a question, make sure you pause before expecting them to respond with an answer. Students need time to process information, reflect on what has been said and consider what their personal response will be. This is particularly important if we are asking our students to do this in a foreign language. Research suggests that students should be given at least three seconds uninterrupted thinking time. This should result in more students contributing and more correct answers. It also demonstrates to our students that we value a thoughtful response. Some teachers are afraid that three seconds of silence feels like a long time but try it and you may be surprised at the difference it makes!

No hands-up

Some teachers have a 'no hands-up' policy in their classroom and select students at random to respond to their question instead. You could ask all your students to write their names on a piece of card and put them in a box. You can then select a student to respond to your question by drawing a name from the box. This ensures that all students are engaged as they may be called upon to answer at any point and prevents certain students dominating. For a 'no hands-up' policy to be effective, the classroom culture needs to be collaborative and supportive. For students to be prepared to take intellectual risks, they need to view mistakes as an inevitable and valuable part of the language learning process.

Pose, pause, pounce, bounce

This is an effective questioning technique to improve the quality of responses you get from students as well as promoting engagement.

- **Pose** a question to the class.
- **Pause** to give all students time to consider their answer.
- **Pounce** on one student to answer the question.
- **Bounce** the question to another student. The second student needs to acknowledge the first student's answer and build on it.

Think-pair-share

When you ask students a question, first give them some individual 'wait time' to consider their answer. Then, let them discuss their answer with a partner before asking them to share their ideas in a larger group or with the whole class. This enables students to order their thoughts before being asked to speak in front of the class and encourages all students to contribute.

Teacher Tip

Students often ask surprisingly few questions, given that they are the ones doing the learning. Encourage your students to come up with their own questions about a particular topic.

Giving effective feedback

The questioning techniques and activities discussed so far provide us with powerful feedback about where our students are in the learning process. We now need to think about the nature of the feedback we provide our students as well as the feedback students can offer each other. It's important that feedback focuses on the qualities of students' work and provides specific advice on how they can improve. With this in mind, it's helpful to think about the following questions.

When do we give feedback?

We know that feedback should form an integral part of the lesson and that the more immediate the feedback is, the better. Some of the questioning techniques discussed so far in this chapter allow us to understand students' thinking and provide immediate feedback: *Why do you think that? Can you give me another example?*

If you are focusing on fluency rather than accuracy in a speaking activity, you might decide to monitor students as they discuss a topic in pairs or groups and then record any errors you have noted down on the board at the end for the class to correct together. This means that you are not interrupting the flow of students' discussions and you can make a decision about which errors you think are worth focusing on at that point in your teaching. Being selective about which errors you focus on ensures that you're not over-correcting your students and discouraging them from experimenting with new language or from even using the language at all.

For some activities, it's helpful to correct mistakes as soon as they are made. Support students to take some responsibility for error correction and encourage them to pick up constructively on each other's mistakes.

You might decide to design a quick quiz for the beginning of the next lesson, based on common errors that you picked up during class. This will consolidate what students have learned and help them to avoid repeating the same mistakes.

Watch out for students repeatedly making the same mistakes – when incorrect language becomes a habit, it is very difficult to correct. If the error doesn't hinder communication, it is often overlooked. Get students to record themselves speaking and listen back; they'll often spot their own mistakes more readily when encouraged to focus in this way on the language they produce.

Teacher Tip

Remind your students that if they are making new mistakes, this is a sign that they are exploring new language which is a necessary part of how we learn. Ask them to dedicate some space in their notebooks to record their errors and the correction. This enables students to keep a track of their progress and helps them to avoid repeating the same mistakes.

Who gives the feedback?

We should be aiming for our students to become confident enough that they can assess each other's work as well as their own. Students will often accept comments from each other more readily than from the teacher and, in addition, the exchanges are in a language students are familiar with. When an activity has been completed, ask students to exchange work and comment on what their partner has done well in relation to the success criteria, and what they could do to make their work even better. If peer-assessment is new to your class, it's helpful to give them a framework and model of how to give good feedback and make constructive suggestions. Many teachers use the 'two stars, one wish' approach to get their students to focus on two strengths and one area for development.

Alternatively, students could use a mark scheme (which you need to negotiate with them at the beginning of the task) to form the basis for their discussions about progress and feedback to their peers.

Teacher Tip

Students need to learn how to assess each other's work meaningfully. If your students are new to peer-assessment, introduce them to the idea by using a sample piece of work and rehearse giving and receiving feedback with them. This helps to build confidence and trust before expecting students to apply the techniques to each other's work.

You could also ask students to work together to reach an agreement about what works well and where the areas for improvement are. Ask students to discuss one piece of work at a time in pairs, focusing on strengths and areas for improvement. This discussion often leads to a close analysis of the work that has been produced. Ultimately, students are aiming to reach an agreement so that the owner of the work can then record the feedback and make improvements. In Chapter 8 **Metacognition**, we will explore in greater depth how to support students when reflecting on and assessing their own work.

🔲 LESSON IDEA ONLINE 7.3: PEER ASSESSMENT FEEDBACK

Lesson idea 7.3 helps you to structure a discussion among your students to ensure they feel confident in providing meaningful feedback to their partner to help them improve.

Figure 7.4

What do we expect our students to do with the feedback?

The impact of feedback is lessened if we don't expect students to do anything with it. Feedback should encourage students to think and prompt them to take action, so it is important that we allow time for this. If you provide feedback on students' homework, make sure you create an expectation that they respond to that feedback. Some teachers ask students to record areas for improvement on the top of their next piece of work before they start, or to build in lesson time to respond to comments. Others expect students to repeat a task taking feedback into account.

Consider giving students feedback without accompanying it with a mark. As soon as you include a mark, this is what students focus on, ignoring the important information about how they can improve.

▣ LESSON IDEA ONLINE 7.4: FEEDBACK CODES
Lesson idea 7.4 introduces students to the idea of feedback codes. You can use them to encourage students to reflect on their work and correct their mistakes to improve their language use.

Summary

- Know where your students are starting from and identify any gaps in understanding before continuing.

- Set clear learning goals and share them with students.

- Make sure students understand what success for that learning goal looks like.

- Ask questions and set tasks that generate evidence of learning.

- Provide feedback that challenges students to think, which in turn, prompts action.

Metacognition

8

What is metacognition?

Metacognition describes the processes involved when students plan, monitor, evaluate and make changes to their own learning behaviours. These processes help students to think about their own learning more explicitly and ensure that they are able to meet a learning goal that they have identified themselves or that we, as teachers, have set.

Metacognitive learners recognise what they find easy or difficult. They understand the demands of a particular learning task and are able to identify different approaches they could use to tackle a problem. Metacognitive learners are also able to make adjustments to their learning as they monitor their progress towards a particular learning goal.

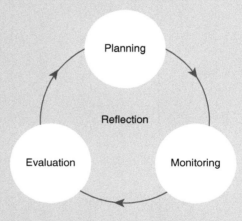

Figure 8.1: A helpful way to think about the phases involved in metacognition.

During the *planning* phase, students think about the explicit learning goal we have set and what we are asking them to do. As teachers, we need to make clear to students what success looks like in any given task before they embark on it. Students build on their prior knowledge, reflect on strategies they have used before and consider how they will approach the new task.

As students put their plan into action, they are constantly *monitoring* the progress they are making towards their learning goal. If the strategies they had decided to use are not working, they may decide to try something different.

Once they have completed the task, students determine how successful the strategy they used was in helping them to achieve their learning goal. During this *evaluation* phase, students think about what went well and what didn't go as well to help them decide what they could do differently next time. They may also think about what other types of problems they could solve using the same strategy.

Reflection is a fundamental part of the plan–monitor–evaluate process and there are various ways in which we can support our students to reflect on their learning process. In order to apply a metacognitive approach, students need access to a set of strategies that they can use and a classroom environment that encourages them to explore and develop their metacognitive skills.

Why teach metacognitive skills?

Research evidence suggests that the use of metacognitive skills plays an important role in successful learning. Metacognitive practices help students to monitor their own progress and take control of their learning. Metacognitive learners think about and learn from their mistakes and modify their learning strategies accordingly. Students who use metacognitive techniques find it improves their academic achievement across subjects, as it helps them transfer what they have learnt from one context to another context, or from a previous task to a new task.

What are the challenges of developing students' metacognitive skills?

For metacognition to be commonplace in the classroom, we need to encourage students to take time to think about and learn from their mistakes. Many students are afraid to make mistakes, meaning that they are less likely to take risks, explore new ways of thinking or tackle unfamiliar problems. We as teachers are instrumental in shaping the culture of learning in a classroom. For metacognitive practices to thrive, students need to feel confident enough to make mistakes, to discuss their mistakes and ultimately to view them as valuable, and often necessary, learning opportunities.

Developing linguists

Students may have limited exposure to the target language in school, but hopefully their language learning will continue outside the classroom. In an increasingly global world, students may travel, study or work abroad and their language skills will continue to develop. To help our students to grow as successful linguists in whichever languages become important in their lives, we need to support them to understand and take responsibility for how they learn best.

Planning for learning

As we discussed in Chapter 7 **Assessment for Learning**, we need to ensure that our students understand the learning goal we have set and what success in that learning goal looks like before they embark on a task. Only once they are clear about where they are going, can they begin planning how best to get there.

For students, this process of planning should include considering what they already know, and which strategies they can apply when approaching a new task.

Activating prior learning

The first stage in a lesson should help students to activate any knowledge they may already have, relevant experience and skills they might need to be successful. In terms of prior knowledge, this might be topic-specific vocabulary, particular grammatical structures or cultural understanding that will be useful for the upcoming task. We want to create a context in which our students are able to connect any new learning to what they already know.

LESSON IDEA ONLINE 8.1: KWL CHART

Lesson idea 8.1 uses a KWL chart to help students organise information before, during and after a lesson or unit of learning. It helps engage students in a new topic, activate their prior knowledge and support them in monitoring their learning.

What I know	What I want to know	What I learned

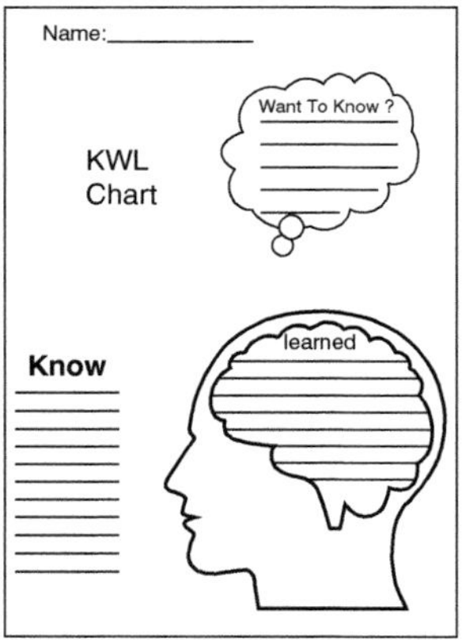

Figure 8.2

To help students to begin thinking about what they already know, and to enable them to complete the first (K) section of their KWL chart, some of the following techniques might be useful.

Predicting

Present students with a stimulus that provides a clue as to the focus of the activity they will be doing. Then ask them what they think they might be reading, writing, listening or speaking about. This might be a photograph or cartoon, just the headline of an article or a video clip of a news report with no sound, or simply a question formulated by you and posed to the whole class. You might want to discuss the understanding of particular concepts and knowledge in their L1(first language) before moving onto activating the target language.

Language generation

Begin by posing a question or introducing a topic. Give pairs or groups of students a designated amount of time to generate as many words, phrases or ideas as they can relate to the topic in the target language. Ask them to put each word or phrase on a single sticky label. Once the time is up, ask students to move to look at another group's labels and make a note of any good ideas they can add to their own list. To extend this activity, ask students to return to their original list and categorise their labels, encouraging them to make connections. These connections might be between language forms or concepts and ideas – let them decide.

Matching

Ask students to match words with pictures, with their definitions or with the correct translation, for example, or matching two halves of a sentence. To activate knowledge of grammar rules, you could ask them to match verb stems with the correct endings.

Put a choice of two verb endings on the board and ask students to choose one and justify their choice. In pairs, ask students to recall the rules for the specific grammar point and write these down.

Teacher Tip

During the planning phase, it's helpful to encourage students to ask themselves:

What am I being asked to do?

Which strategies will I use?

Are there any strategies that I have used before that might be useful?

Modelling strategies

The most successful students are those who are able to think about the strategies available to them, monitor how successful they are, and consider trying something different if the strategy they have chosen isn't working. In language teaching in particular, there are a wide range of strategies to scaffold students' learning in the four skills of Reading, Writing, Speaking and Listening. But for students to be able to successfully identify strategies, we need to be explicit about which ones we are using, when we are using them and why they are successful.

Giving strategies names or acronyms facilitates discussion about their use. For example:

- **Reading:** reading for gist
- **Writing:** creating a writing frame
- **Speaking:** recycling structures
- **Listening:** predicting language

Students may prefer to use different strategies so it's a good idea to discuss strategy selection with them as well as encourage them to discuss what they are doing with each other.

LESSON IDEA 8.2: THINKING ALOUD

Thinking aloud is a strategy where teachers verbalise their thoughts and students can follow the teacher's thinking process. In turn, this helps students to establish their own useful strategies for consciously monitoring what they are learning and reflecting on *how* they are learning it. When you are planning your next lesson:

- identify a skill that you want to teach or revisit (e.g. correctly forming the perfect tense for regular *'er'* verbs in French.)
- choose a specific example (i.e. a simple sentence that doesn't introduce unnecessary new vocabulary that will distract from the focus).
- decide the steps needed to complete the task (e.g. choose the verb you want to use, *remove* the *'er'*, add an *é*, decide whether it takes *avoir* or *être*, choose the correct form of the auxiliary verb in the present tense, add the chosen past participle, etc.)
- plan a think-aloud script. (In your script include things like: asking yourself questions, weighing up alternatives and self-correction.)

Before you start your thinking-aloud task with your students, explain why you are doing it and what you want them to learn. Once you have modelled the skill using the think-aloud technique, ask your students to identify the strategies or the steps you took. Clearly record the steps and display them somewhere for students to refer to in the future.

Put the students into groups and ask them to solve a problem using the steps that you have just modelled. Encourage them to think aloud in their groups as they solve the problem so that they can give each other feedback about whether they have correctly followed the steps.

Monitoring progress

When students are completing a task, they need to consider how well the strategy they are using is working and to try something different if necessary. For example, you have asked a student to answer a series of multiple-choice questions based on a listening exercise. The first strategy the student tries (1) is to listen to the audio once and make a note of all the details they hear. However, this doesn't work as there are too many things to note down and they quickly get lost.

The student decides to try a different strategy (2). Before listening for a second time, they read the questions and underline key words, without looking at the options for answers. They listen and make notes based on what they have underlined, listen a third time and then choose the option.

This strategy works better. However, the next time they do a multiple-choice listening exercise, the student decides to try something different (3), they underline the key words in the question and also read through options underlining key words. They listen and only note down key words next to the options. They listen a second time and then choose the option.

Different students will find different strategies useful. Our aim is to make students aware of the strategies they are using and to encourage them to consider which is most effective in a given task. It's useful to pause mid-task and ask students to share with each other which strategies they are using.

Teacher Tip

To ensure students continually monitor their progress, it's helpful to encourage them to ask themselves:

How am I doing?

Is the strategy that I am using working?

Do I need to try something different?

If we ensure students have a range of strategies at their disposal, we can help to prevent them from panicking or feeling anxious when they are presented with new, unfamiliar language and tasks. They will hopefully see it as a welcome challenge and set about thinking how best they can solve the puzzle. Emphasising that there isn't necessarily a 'right' way to approach a new linguistic challenge also encourages students to take risks and to try something new if their approach isn't working rather than simply giving up.

> ☑ **LESSON IDEA ONLINE 8.3: CLOZE READING**
>
> Lesson idea 8.3 helps students to focus on specific aspects of language and at the same time highlights the reading strategies they are using.

Taking risks

Metacognitive learners think about and learn from their mistakes. In order for you to be able to establish metacognitive practices with your students, you need to encourage them to feel confident enough to make mistakes and to take the time to reflect on and learn from these mistakes. Students can find learning a language difficult and at times it can be frustrating when they feel they can't effectively communicate their ideas. It's important that we make it clear to our students that we expect them to experiment with language, make decisions that may not always be correct, and keep trying in order to succeed.

Mistakes provide us with the necessary feedback that we need to improve and this is particularly true for language learning. We expect to hear children making mistakes in their first language as they develop (an example of this might be applying a principle of regular change to an irregular verb), and we should expect the same from our students as they try out new words and structures. If students always feel they have to wait until they have formulated a grammatically sound sentence before they are prepared to say it or write it down, then progress will be slow. But this feeling of being transported back to a stage where you struggle to communicate what you have in your mind can be inhibiting. It's our job to create a classroom culture in which students not only feel comfortable being challenged and taking risks but are actively encouraged to do so (we look at this in more detail in Chapter 9 **Inclusive education**). Set the example, model making mistakes and self-correcting, and verbalise your thought process as you do it so that students can follow. All teachers need to keep up-to-date with their subject knowledge and language is no exception – it's always evolving. Don't be afraid to let your students know that you're going to check something or do some more research yourself.

Getting stuck

Students develop resilience when they are given problems that are challenging but not impossible. We are learning to persevere when we get stuck on a problem. Metacognitive students are constantly monitoring their progress towards their learning goal and if the strategies they are using are not working, they don't give up, they try something different. Establish high expectations for your students and let them know you are challenging them because they can succeed and that you value learning and effort above performance.

Feedback on the process of learning

Give your students specific feedback on the different strategies they are using and how effective they are. This focuses on the process of learning and encourages systematic evaluation and reflection from your students about how they learn. For example, you might recognise that a student has misunderstood the meaning of a text and you suspect that this is because they have translated the text word for word. You could prompt them to reflect on the strategy they used to interpret the meaning of the text and consider what they could do differently next time, such as skimming the text to first get an overall sense of the meaning and using visual clues to predict content.

When we offer students feedback on their metacognitive skills, we are demonstrating that this is something we consider important and of value. As we encourage students to take risks and try out new language, highlight those students who are learning from their mistakes and self-correcting (see some examples in Figure 8.3).

Figure 8.3

Evaluating learning

It's important to build systematic opportunities for evaluation in our lessons. Support students to consider what went well and perhaps what didn't go as well in order to help them to decide what to do differently next time. Here are a few ideas to try:

Exam wrappers

Exam wrappers are worksheets containing reflective questions that help students to review their performance in a test. Exam wrappers can be given to students both before and after they receive the results of the test and feedback. Worksheets handed out before receiving feedback prompt the student to reflect on how they prepared for the exam including the study strategies they used. A worksheet handed out after the student has received the test feedback, might ask them to review the feedback, to categorise any errors made and reflect on how they can prepare differently for the next assessment. These worksheets can be adapted and used for any task – not just exams.

Teacher Tip

To help students to evaluate their learning after completing a task, it's helpful to encourage students to ask themselves:

How well did I do?

What went well? What other types of problem can I use this strategy for?

What didn't go well? What could I do differently next time?

Learning journals

One way to help students monitor their own progress is through the use of personal learning journals. Assign weekly questions that are designed to support students to reflect on how, rather than what, they've learnt. Questions might include:

- What did I find easiest to learn this week? Why?
- What did I find most challenging this week? Why?
- What study strategies worked well?
- How did I continue my language learning outside the classroom?
- What study habit will I try to improve for next week?

Students can choose to keep learning journals in a variety of ways and you might encourage them to be creative by choosing any type of format they prefer, such as mind maps, blogs, wikis, diaries and social media sites. Make sure it's a format they can share with you.

Summary

- Activate students' prior knowledge so that they connect new learning to what they already know and are able to do.

- Ensure students are clear about the learning goal and success criteria for a task so that they can plan how best to approach it.

- Model and discuss the use of different strategies with your students and encourage them to do the same.

- Support students to monitor their progress while they are completing a task, giving them the opportunity to try something different if what they are doing isn't working.

- Make mistakes and learn from them – encourage your students to do the same.

- Recognise students for asking questions, get them to explain their reasoning and reflect on their and others' approaches to a task.

Inclusive
education

9

What is inclusive education?

Individual differences among students will always exist; our challenge as teachers is to see these not as problems to be fixed but as opportunities to enrich and make learning accessible for all. Inclusion is an effort to make sure all students receive whatever specially designed instruction and support they need to succeed as learners.

An inclusive teacher welcomes all students and finds ways to accept and accommodate each individual student. An inclusive teacher identifies existing barriers that limit access to learning, then finds solutions and strategies to remove or reduce those barriers. Some barriers to inclusion are visible; others are hidden or difficult to recognise.

Barriers to inclusion might be the lack of educational resources available for teachers or an inflexible curriculum that does not take into account the learning differences that exist among all learners, across all ages. We also need to encourage students to understand each others' barriers, or this itself may become a barrier to learning.

Students may experience challenges because of any one or a combination of the following:

- behavioural and social skill difficulties
- communication or language disabilities
- concentration difficulties
- conflict in the home or that caused by political situations or national emergency
- executive functions, such as difficulties in understanding, planning and organising
- hearing impairments, acquired congenitally or through illness or injury
- literacy and language difficulties
- numeracy difficulties
- physical or neurological impairments, which may or may not be visible
- visual impairments, ranging from mild to severe.

We should be careful, however, not to label a student and create further barriers in so doing, particularly if we ourselves are not qualified to make a diagnosis. Each student is unique but it is our management of their learning environment that will decide the extent of the barrier and the need for it to be a factor. We need to be aware of a student's readiness to learn and their readiness for school.

Why is inclusive education important?

Teachers need to find ways to welcome all students and organise their teaching so that each student gets a learning experience that makes engagement and success possible. We should create a good match between what we teach and how we teach it, and what the student needs and is capable of. We need not only to ensure access but also make sure each student receives the support and individual attention that result in meaningful learning.

What are the challenges of an inclusive classroom?

Some students may have unexpected barriers. Those who consistently do well in class may not perform in exams, or those who are strong at writing may be weaker when speaking. Those who are considered to be the brightest students may also have barriers to learning. Some students may be working extra hard to compensate for barriers they prefer to keep hidden; some students may suddenly reveal limitations in their ability to learn, using the techniques they have been taught. We need to be aware of all corners of our classroom, be open and put ourselves in our students' shoes.

Looking in the mirror

Each and every one of us will have experienced times when we have felt excluded or different to other people. Each and every one of us as teachers of Modern Foreign Languages will have met challenges in our learning and understanding of vocabulary, grammar and even culture. If we have been successful in our language learning, we will have found ways to overcome, work around or work with these challenges on our own or with some dedicated help.

In each of the classes we teach we will see students, each of whom is an individual, with their own background and experiences, their own ways of thinking, preferred ways of learning, and their own challenges. As teachers, it is our role to try to include all students in our lessons. We are there to support them all, to raise their aspirations and to unlock their potential. If we begin with a positive attitude and talk in terms of 'differences', rather than 'difficulties', we will meet with more hopes than fears.

Teacher Tip

Be honest and reflect on your own learning experiences: what do you find challenging about the foreign language that you teach? Perhaps you struggle with a certain tense or with spelling certain words? Perhaps you regularly confuse two languages you know? What techniques have you used or discovered to help you? And what about the culture of the countries where the language you teach is spoken? Is there anything you find challenging to accept or is there anything you find particularly liberating? You can put yourself more easily in your students' shoes if you can try and look objectively at yourself.

Languages for all

In some schools it is the policy for students who have been diagnosed with specific learning differences not to learn Modern Foreign Languages. If they find aspects of their own language or the language of instruction challenging, students are often sent to other classes when they might otherwise be studying our subject. There can be good and sensible reasons for this, but not always. It may in fact be that learning another language gives them the boost they need.

Just because a student has been designated as dyslexic, hyperactive, autistic, it does not necessarily follow that they do not have the capacity to learn a foreign language. It may in fact play to that student's strengths and talents, and in some cases it may allow them to invent a new persona, to invent a 'foreign' self and so thrive in an environment where they feel more at home. A student may find learning a new language a new opportunity to understand language in general.

Think of the student who finds Writing or Reading difficult. Many students who you think are fluent in English often come unstuck when they are being asked to put pen to paper.

Figure 9.1: Overcoming and dealing with barriers.

This in fact is often also a way of spotting the student who may be dyslexic, as there can be quite a discrepancy between the quality of their oral and written work. Will the student who is dyslexic in English be dyslexic in all languages?

In our experience, sometimes students who are dyslexic appear to cope better with languages that are spelt phonetically (e.g. German) or with characters (e.g. Mandarin Chinese). Bear in mind, though, that some students (and maybe you) will find languages written in other ways quite a challenge. If you teach a language which uses a different way of writing, think carefully how best to engage students in this challenge, perhaps playing to their artistic talents or skills for spotting patterns.

As in any teaching, it is important to help students construct their learning. You need to prepare them to use the alphabet or characters of the foreign language and it is time well spent early on. Think of the times when you have asked students to read out loud or to listen to what you are saying and they have misheard or misinterpreted the simplest of words. A student who has solid foundations with regard to pronunciation will have a head start.

LESSON IDEA 9.1: SPELLING TEST
Instead of giving your students vocabulary tests, surprise them with a spelling test. You could also do this in combination with flashcards showing an image of the word you are spelling. Invite one student to ask another to spell a word while another finds the relevant flashcard. Prepare the test carefully, starting with shorter words and focusing on particular letters or letter combinations.

As students progress with the foreign language, expose them to other accents and intonations. It wasn't until my A Level Listening exam that I heard for the first time someone from North Africa speaking French and rolling the letter 'r'. It was much later that I got to compare the way the language is spoken in Canada, Switzerland and West Africa. It can't be over-emphasised enough how important it is, wherever possible, to attune students' ears to a foreign language.

Teacher Tip

If you are teaching a Romance language, focus above all on the vowels and diphthongs, which are often a key part of pronunciation. Make your students aware too of how letters might sound different because of other letters that precede or follow them. Once students are confident about how to pronounce letters, try dictating short phrases or sentences for them to write. Maintain regular focus on pronunciation in a variety of ways, with an element of fun. For example, give students a paragraph to learn to pronounce as perfectly as they can and choose or ask for volunteers to compete in a friendly and supportive way to see who is best.

Creating the right conditions

As you will have seen throughout this book, a lot of teaching is about creating the conditions for learning to take place. The first lessons you have with a new group of students will set the tone for what follows, so it is a good idea to plan them carefully. Think about the layout of your classroom, where you ask students to sit – especially if they find it hard to see, hear, or concentrate, what equipment you expect them to bring to lessons, and what notes you want them to take.

One of my best teachers taught me Latin. In the first week, he gave us two medium-sized exercise books and two half-size exercise books. One of the larger exercise books was for doing language work, such as practising sentences or doing translations, and the other was for taking notes or writing essays about Roman culture and history. One of the smaller books was for vocabulary and the other was carefully designed by him page-by-page to make particular notes on grammar.

I credit this teacher with providing me with the structure and clarity to pursue my learning of the language for the following seven years and perhaps also for encouraging my approach to and love of learning any language. He set us up for success by thinking carefully about the key points he wanted us to learn and in what precise way he wanted us to record them. He set himself up for success too, by making it easy to mark our work and know when we had done as we had been told!

Figure 9.2: Students often need help in organising their notes.

We are not suggesting that this method will work for everyone, but the point to take away here is that we should not assume that our students know how to learn a language, how to note down what we teach them or how to revise what is in the syllabus. Many of our students will never have learnt a language before including, as we have alluded to above, their own, in the sense of studying its grammar. We need to get the basics right before we can help them to succeed.

In time, students will establish their own preferences for how to learn, and it is important to give them this freedom as they take greater responsibility for their work. As we saw in Chapter 8 **Metacognition** though, we still need to check regularly on what they are doing and how they are doing it. If they are struggling with a particular aspect of language learning, it may mean that the method they are using needs attention and a small change would make all the difference.

Teacher Tip

If you haven't set the rules for how students record what they are learning, ask them to compare their methods for note-taking with each other and then discuss (as a group) what works well.

While we're thinking about creating the conditions for learning to take place, let's also focus on grammar. Not all the students in your class – and maybe none of them – will know the terminology. As teachers, we need to introduce this jargon carefully, and it is best introduced gradually so we don't discourage students. Our students don't need to recognise every item, but it is important that they can identify nouns, adjectives, verbs and any other terms pertinent to the target language.

Before attending our classes, some students may have had previous experience of the language. We need to determine what grammar they know, where they have gaps and where they might have made (wrong) assumptions about what is correct. A good way of doing this is to devise a cloze exercise where students fill gaps in sentences from a list of words you give them. Depending on the students' level and the language, use a variety of similar verb and adjective endings.

LESSON IDEA 9.2: IDENTIFYING GRAMMATICAL TERMS

Create a short text using vocabulary that your students will know. If your students are working on paper, give them highlighters or coloured pencils; if they are working on computers get them to choose a series of colours. Ask them to go through the text word-by-word and identify the nouns, adjectives, verbs, or any other grammatical item you want them to learn, using a different colour to highlight each item. Don't forget, of course, that not everyone sees colours the same way, which is why it is important to get students to choose the colours themselves.

If the language you are teaching has specific rules that may be different to students' own languages and so a potential barrier, such as adjectives 'agreeing' with nouns, or verb endings 'agreeing' with the person who is initiating (or receiving) the action, you can teach your students how to parse (analyse) a sentence. Students find this surprisingly enjoyable and it often leads to them paying far greater attention to the language they write and to their overall approach to reading.

Having a go

In the days when I was more timid and introverted I used to hate speaking foreign languages. I was very good at reading and writing, not bad at listening, but in oral tests I lacked confidence. Fortunately, I overcame this through encouragement and purposeful practice before I left school and kept improving on my other skills. As a teacher, I have come across students who met the same challenges as me but also others who were always willing and eager to have a go at speaking.

These days we are much more aware of students' social and emotional needs. We need to support, develop and coach students in a way that is appropriate to the needs we identify. The student who appears less confident when talking in front of the class may be more at ease in a pair or group. The student who is bolder may be able to provide encouragement, or may be an obstacle. Create the right conditions for quieter students to gain in confidence and talk out loud when they are ready.

Teacher Tip

Never label a student as 'shy', 'slow', 'disruptive', etc. This will stigmatise the student in your eyes and those of others and will become an additional barrier to learning and teaching. You may fail to notice when the barrier they had is no longer there.

If students are preparing for exams, they will normally have to be tested on their speaking ability. You may need to spend more time with those that find this difficult. Away from assessments, don't forget that many excellent linguists may also be better at writing than speaking. Remember that many jobs exist for those who are good at languages that only involve reading or writing. You may have reluctant speakers who could become translators or code breakers!

Figure 9.3: Students may one day work as interpreters or translators.

Some students may find writing more difficult. This could be because they find this hard in their own language or it could simply be because they are not used to writing much in any language! If you are asking your students to write by hand, think back to the last time you wrote anything in pen or pencil on something bigger than a sticky note. In other words, be sensible about what you are asking students to do. Give them a realistic exercise they can relate to, such as writing a brief social media message.

However, students who are studying for exams and who want to progress in the language will need to learn to write longer texts. As we saw in Chapter 7 **Assessment for Learning**, they will be asked to respond to rubrics and cover certain points for their efforts to gain marks. Focusing on these helps students chunk up and scaffold what they are writing. As with any large task, it is often useful to break it into small parts so that it appears less intimidating and more manageable.

If students are writing long, discursive essays, you need to help them construct these. It can be a challenge for any student to debate an argument on a topic they have never previously thought about. Be mindful of the different backgrounds and experiences of your students when selecting topics, in case some are particularly sensitive. When students study controversial topics, they are often only just forming their opinions of other people and the world around them. Some students may simply not be mature enough.

> **▣ LESSON IDEA ONLINE 9.3: CONSTRUCTING A DISCURSIVE ESSAY**
>
> Lesson idea 9.3 helps students construct essays using chunking and scaffolding techniques.

Reading and Listening, or at least the former, tend to pose fewer problems for most students as they are passive skills. Again, don't forget, however, that many students may not be in the habit of reading, or even listening, especially if they are being asked to complete tasks requiring higher-order thinking. Before they can perform well in these skills, you may need to help them form these habits and gradually build up the length and intensity of what you are expecting your students to do.

Teacher Tip

If you want to be fully inclusive in your lessons, always think of your audience and consider the environment in which they are growing up today. It is possible that you are unwittingly creating more challenges for them by not looking at the world from their perspective. Spend time interacting with or simply listening to them to tune into their hopes and fears.

Assessing inclusively

If you are testing students during or at the end of the year, or if they are working towards high stakes assessments, you need to prepare them: there is little point in setting up your students for failure. You can't just tell your students to revise the language – or even learn from a small vocabulary test. You need to work with them to discover the techniques that work best for them, and these methods may not necessarily be the ones that worked for you.

It is the same if any of your students are given what are commonly known as 'special considerations' in externally assessed exams.

Sometimes, for example, they may be given 25% extra time, someone may be writing on their behalf, or they may use a computer while others write long hand; still others may need prompters who either assist students in keeping track of time or nudge them every so often to keep them focused.

Whatever the special consideration, students need to practise it. What should be different about the way they pace their work if they have extra time? If the language they are studying has accents on letters, do they know how to find these on a computer? If they are given special considerations in externally assessed exams, should they also receive these in formative assessments throughout the year and even in their home or classwork? Your school may have a policy on this.

Teacher Tip

Talk to other teachers about how they assist their students with special considerations. How, for example, do teachers of subjects where students will be required to write essays in timed conditions prepare them to do this?

You may be fortunate enough to have a native speaker language assistant working with you. This person can be very useful when students are preparing for their oral exams. They too will need to know what is being assessed and how, and you will need to work closely with them to ascertain and give positive help to those who have specific needs of whatever nature in their language learning. Few language assistants are trained teachers, making this even more essential.

In oral exams, students often have to perform role-plays. Once again, they may never have found themselves in a situation in their own language where they have had such a conversation, so you need to prepare them appropriately for this. Some students, particularly those who are dyslexic or hyperactive, can revel in assuming different characters or being on stage and surprise you with their linguistic talents. This can be a great opportunity to encourage them and play to their strengths.

Being inclusive

If you are being inclusive, you are essentially allowing every student the opportunity to learn something about the foreign language you teach. Some will be more able or interested than others, but every student can reach a certain level, enjoy what they are learning, and some may even discover a whole new world that appeals to them much more than their current situation. Do seek advice from your special needs coordinator if you have one.

Figure 9.4: Knowing certain words in a foreign language can keep you out of danger.

It can in fact be lifesaving for students to have the basics of the languages of countries they might visit in their lifetimes. Perhaps a student has an allergy to a type of food or animal: it will be important that they know how to express this. What about reading signs that tell of danger, or when water is drinkable? Even being able to tell the time or understand a weather forecast can be useful. Students need to know they cannot always rely on others to speak their language.

Teacher Tip

Have some personal anecdotes to tell your students about times when knowing words in a language got you out of a difficult situation – or when not knowing them got you into trouble! You could also talk about situations where you have been or seen others misled by 'false friends'. This is a good example of personalising language learning to make it more real and relevant. Your own stories will be remembered much more than tales in a textbook.

☑ LESSON IDEA ONLINE 9.4: FRIENDS IN NEED

Lesson idea 9.4 is designed to involve all students. It features a short scenario that students need to investigate about some characters who have got into trouble.

Learning languages, as we will discuss more in Chapter 11 **Global thinking**, encourages open-mindedness. This includes being circumspect about those who may be different for whatever reason. To our students, people who speak other languages and have other cultural backgrounds may appear peculiar but they are part of our shared humanity, and it is one of our roles as language teachers to pass this on. Just as we accept people of other cultures, we should accept all types of student in our language classroom.

Summary

- We all have our own barriers to learning: honesty about this leads us to appreciate how and why other people might be different and the challenges they might face.

- Some barriers are visible, some are hidden: if a student is under- (or over-) performing in a certain skill or area of language learning, there is normally a reason for this that we need to identify and help them manage.

- We should not assume students are ready to do whatever we are asking them to do: we need to create the conditions for learning to take place.

- Not all students will turn out to be strong linguists. They might have other interests or difficulties in processing language. However, they all deserve the opportunity to have a go, and some may even find they can 'reinvent' themselves.

- It can literally be vital for some students, especially those with health problems, to know and be able to communicate some basic words in a foreign language.

Teaching with digital technologies

10

What are digital technologies?

Digital technologies enable our students to access a wealth of up-to-date digital resources, collaborate locally and globally, curate existing material and create new material. They include electronic devices and tools that manage and manipulate information and data.

Why use digital technologies in the classroom?

When used successfully, digital technologies have the potential to transform teaching and learning. The effective use of technology in the classroom encourages active learning, knowledge construction, inquiry and exploration among students. It should enhance an existing task or provide opportunities to do things that could not be done without it. It can also enhance the role of assessment, providing new ways for students to demonstrate evidence of learning.

New technologies are redefining relationships and enabling new opportunities. But there are also risks, so we should encourage our students to be knowledgeable about and responsible in their use of technology. Integrating technology into our teaching helps prepare students for a future rooted in an increasingly digitised world.

What are the challenges of using digital technologies?

The key to ensuring that technology is used effectively is to remember that it is simply a resource, and not an end in itself. As with the use of all resources, the key is not to start with the resource itself, but to start with what you want the student to learn. We need to think carefully about why and how to use technologies as well as evaluating their efficiency and effectiveness.

If students are asked to use digital technologies as part of their homework, it is important that all students are able to access the relevant technology outside school. A school needs to think about a response to any 'digital divide', because if technology is 'adding value', then all students need to be able to benefit. Some schools choose to make resources available to borrow or use in school, or even loan devices to students.

Safety for students and teachers is a key challenge for schools and it is important to consider issues such as the prevention of cyber-bullying, the hacking of personal information, access to illegal or banned materials and distractions from learning. As technology changes, schools and teachers need to adapt and implement policies and rules.

One of the greatest pitfalls is for a teacher to feel that they are not skilled technologists, and therefore not to try. Creative things can be done with simple technology, and a highly effective teacher who knows very little about technology can often achieve much more than a less effective teacher who is a technology expert. Knowing how to use technology is not the same as knowing how to teach with it.

Back to the future

My degree in Modern Foreign Languages gave me plenty of vocabulary with which to communicate about literature and 20th century culture. All my studies and research were done in books and in buildings called libraries; it was only in my final year that I sent my very first email. I am what Marc Prensky, in his 2001 journal article, *On the Horizon*, termed a 'digital immigrant'. Perhaps you fall into this category too – but today's students are and always will be 'digital natives.'

Prensky goes on to assert that, 'Today's students are no longer the people our educational system was designed to teach.' Whether we embrace modern technology or are inclined to do the opposite, one of our duties as teachers is to prepare students for the world in which they are growing up, not the one that existed when we were at school. We need to coordinate our efforts so that our students will not only be digital natives but also digitally literate.

Figure 10.1: A digital native helping a digital immigrant.

In this chapter, we explore what this means for the way we teach and some key considerations when using technology with students. We will look at how we can learn with and from our students, how the digital world is even larger than the one opened up to us when we first chose to study another language. We will also reflect on when not to use technology and our responsibility in helping students navigate the digital world securely.

Teacher Tip

Before we go any further, give yourself a vocabulary test. List a couple of dozen words in your first language specific to the digital world (e.g. smartphone, search engine, to tweet) and write down their equivalent in the modern foreign language you teach. Like me, you may need a more up-to-date dictionary than the one sitting on your shelf to check your answers! You may also find that some words don't (yet) exist in other languages or that there is currently more than one way of saying the same thing (formally or colloquially).

In the classroom

Let's look first of all at why we might want to use technology. The main question to ask yourself when you prepare any lesson is what is the educational purpose of what you are doing. Don't get tempted by the novelty of the latest gadget, or by a new tool that might subdue and distract your students for a while from behaving badly: focus instead on the impact that the technology will have on learning. Pick the best tool for the best lesson you can teach.

A neat way to help you work out when and where to use technology is the model popularised by Dr Ruben Puentedura known as SAMR. This model takes us from simply enhancing learning and teaching to transforming it through technology (Figure 10.2).

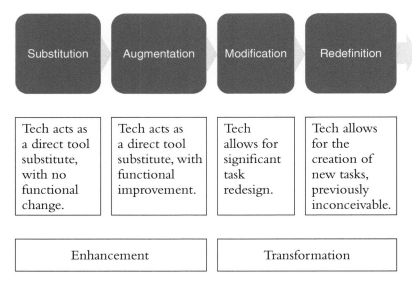

Substitution	Augmentation	Modification	Redefinition
Tech acts as a direct tool substitute, with no functional change.	Tech acts as a direct tool substitute, with functional improvement.	Tech allows for significant task redesign.	Tech allows for the creation of new tasks, previously inconceivable.

Enhancement	Transformation

Figure 10.2: SAMR.

☑ LESSON IDEA ONLINE 10.1: SAMR

Lesson idea 10.1 is an example of how the SAMR model can work in a Modern Foreign Languages lesson.

Jen Roberts, in her blog quoted by Kathy Schrock, has further developed the SAMR model into the more memorable 'TECH' (Traditional, Enhanced, Choice, Handoff). Students are first asked (in the third stage) to choose from a range of tools before taking charge in the fourth stage ('Handoff') of their own learning experience, with guidance from their teacher. In this model we can easily see how the use of technology can help lessons move from being teacher- to student-centred.

☑ LESSON IDEA ONLINE 10.2: TECH

Lesson idea 10.2 is an example of how the TECH model can work in a Modern Foreign Languages lesson.

Teacher Tip

There are many excellent blogs and websites about using technology in education. Bookmark your favourites for future reference and keep up-to-date with what's new. If you're not sure where to start, ask your colleagues – not necessarily those who also teach languages – what they have discovered.

Whatever technology you are using, it's a good idea to practise in advance what you specifically will be doing – and also to have a plan B for when the technology doesn't work or when things go wrong. In the pre-digital age, I once had to put my acting skills on stage in a lesson being observed by a school inspector when a tape player broke down during a listening comprehension exercise and I had to read the parts of the characters in several different voices!

It is also sensible to learn properly how to use technology, ranging from how something switches on and off, to best practice in using certain software. This may sound basic but it is surprising how often teachers give a bad impression. Worksheets that you produce should be clear, neat and error-free; audio and video recordings should be high-quality and not fuzzy or distorted; and presentations, for example, using PowerPoint®, should be designed well and with your audience in mind.

If the language you are teaching has accents or special letters – and even more so if you are teaching a language that uses different characters – you should familiarise yourself with how to find these on a keyboard. On some devices, for example, you can hold a key and options appear; on others you may have to use a toolbar menu or hold 'Alt' while you type in numbers. Pass on to your students how to do this too.

Your students will often, of course, know how to use certain digital tools better than you. They may be more likely to have a growth mindset with regard to technology, more time and motivation to practise using it, and be more likely to persevere. Technology gives us more opportunities to collaborate with our students and co-construct their (and our) learning. Why not invite students to be 'digital champions' for Modern Foreign Languages and assist in lesson design?

You will need to adhere to your school policy with regard to this, but how might your lessons be enhanced if students are encouraged to bring in their own device? Depending on where you live, it may be that students will have better equipment than the school can afford. Students will normally look after their own devices, keep them charged and updated, and also be able to access them at home. Remember, of course, that students without their own devices may need support.

Teacher Tip

Check the digital policy for your school or make sure one is created, if it hasn't done so already. You must be particularly careful about the use of data and images, and be aware of potential menaces online. Get to know what to look out for and how to report any dangers.

Set expectations for how devices will be used. Some teachers shy away from using technology because they fear they will lose control but, just as for any other form of classroom management, you need to establish rules and stick to them. If students are finding it hard to put down their devices or might be distracted by social media during class, you need either to ensure your lesson is more engaging or not permit technology at all.

Ensure you are clear in the educational purpose of what you are doing, expectations are set, and all the equipment is working. Let's take a look at some of the ways in which digital technology can make a big difference to your teaching of Modern Foreign Languages.

- **Differentiate:** You will note that some students work better or more quickly with digital technology than others. When they are ready, invite them to choose their preferred method for learning (while also ensuring they try out alternatives too). This works well if you can set up a carousel of activities on a particular topic or aspect of learning. Students can choose to work alone, in pairs, or in groups to complete a task with or without technology before moving on.
- **Visualisers:** At a more basic level, you can use an overhead (light or camera) projector to show or demonstrate, but digital tools via

computers, tablets and interactive whiteboards widen the scope for analysing work with students. Collectively, you can study a grammar point in a sentence, work through an example essay or look at an exam question. You can also study cultural artefacts or even virtually visit a location together. Try synching your students' devices with your own, using a tool such as Nearpod.

- **Sharing work and resources**: Again, there are many ways of doing this, but some means are proving more popular than others. Fundamentally, it is a very good idea to set up an online 'cloud' space where you can share materials with your colleagues, students and possibly even their parents. You can control privacy settings to decide who can access what, where and when. Examples are Google Apps for Education (the G Suite), Edmodo and Seesaw.
- **Digital templates**: Set up frames to help students in their writing. This could range from close guidance on what needs to be in a sentence (e.g. subject – verb – object) to tips on how to construct an essay. If a student has never previously written anything substantial in the language, they will find a template a helpful starting point and some carefully designed scaffolding will establish a routine of how to approach writing creatively. You could save these on an online platform for students to access easily.
- **Formative assessment**: There are many websites and apps that are simple to use if you want to gauge your students' learning. These include vocabulary or grammar flashcards and quizzes you (or your students) can create yourself using tools such as Kahoot, Quizlet and Memrise, to dedicated online testing programmes. Many of these will allow you to enter students' names and keep track of their scores. Remember to analyse strengths as well as weaknesses.
- **Photos and videos**: Smartphones and tablets are particularly effective at bringing everyday vocabulary and situations to life – they are great for individual, pair or group work. Invite students to go on a treasure hunt around the school or where they live, taking photos of specific items or locations. Later, you could ask them to create, act out and film role-plays or interviews. Get them to collate what they discover and produce electronic scrapbooks or blogs to document their language learning.
- **Virtual reality**: VR is still relatively new in classrooms, but technology giants are investing lots in its research and development, and affordable options already exist. Through technology such as Google Cardboard and its companion Expeditions app, students can be transported to foreign cities and

museums to experience in virtual reality where the language they are learning is spoken. YouTube 360 videos can also bring the outside world to your classroom. While YouTube can be a useful resource, make sure to supervise your students to ensure that they do not access any inappropriate content.

You may also want to use digital technology to enhance how you teach in other ways. If you find it time-consuming to give written feedback (or if your handwriting is deteriorating because of all the typing you do), try giving audio feedback instead. Until it becomes commonplace, this can be a novel experience for your students and they may be more inclined to take note of what you say rather than just focusing on their grade. Try it in the target language when students are ready.

Websites such as Kaizena are worth exploring as they provide a platform for storing comments, for conversing with students about their work, and a repository where you can post videos or presentations on the key concepts you want students to learn. Students can get into the routine of visiting the site regularly to revise what they have covered, catch up on work they have missed, or look back on how much they have advanced in the course of their studies.

Teacher Tip

If you are giving audio feedback in the language you are teaching, it may be better to do so on video so that your students can also look for visual clues – and, if you can, transcribe subtitles as well.

Out of the classroom

We can access an infinite range of resources outside our classrooms and the lessons we teach. It is hard to know where to start unless colleagues have recommended certain websites, tools or digital technologies. It is hard too to remember where you have looked up or spotted something and therefore essential that you get into good habits about tagging and record keeping. Sites such as Diigo and del.icio.us provide platforms for social bookmarking.

It is generally a good idea in any case to keep on top of your filing and curating. Talk to colleagues and also to your students about setting up class or department websites, using social media or wiki pages where resources can be stored and you can create an online community. We need to set an example for students so that they can learn the skills to be 'information literate'. It is one thing to find items on messy bookshelves but quite another to trawl through disorganised digital resources!

Figure 10.3: This is how your computer files might look too if you don't keep them in order!

If you have an online platform specific to the language you teach, get students into the habit of using the appropriate vocabulary when they are searching for or saving items. If they see such words on a regular basis they will soon get to know and remember them. Keep checking too that nobody is lazy in their use of accents or special characters, but above all create a vibrant online environment so that students can see that the language they are learning is also very much alive in the digital world.

You certainly need to plan in advance and organise resources if you are going to ask your students to do work prior to or after a lesson. When students are more advanced in their study of languages, you can try 'flipped learning': this involves asking students to complete some specific learning in their own time before you give them individual attention in class. You could, for example, invite them to translate a blog, view a TED talk, or listen to a foreign radio show.

Students may be inspired to create their own blogs, record their own presentations, or even broadcast their own audio recordings. The tools exist for them to do this and they may already have learnt how in other subjects or as a hobby. If this is a step too far, you may want to encourage them first to tweet (for real or not). You can set up templates for them to do this and you may even want to establish your own departmental (foreign language) Twitter feed.

Teacher Tip

Have a pile of 140-square grids in your classroom (20 columns by 7 rows works best). Each week when you meet your students for the first time, ask them to write in the grid a 140-character 'tweet' about something interesting they have seen or done since they were last with you.

And we mustn't forget how much easier it is today to communicate with people in other countries than it was in the days of sending letters to pen pals! Email exchanges are so much more rapid, as are text and instant messaging services. It is also very simple, if you have the appropriate devices and broadband speeds, to meet students and teachers from other schools via video for free online interaction. In many ways, there is little excuse for not bringing the outside world into your classroom.

As mentioned earlier, you must follow your school's policy with regard to internet use. Seek advice if you are unsure. This can be particularly problematic when students might be exploring websites in another language, as they can easily get lost or go astray. It works the other way too: a school where I once worked banned online chat rooms and in so doing prevented us from searching the words *chat* ('cat') and *château* ('castle') in French!

Maintaining your own language skills

Digital technology provides a fantastic means of keeping up with the language you are teaching and its culture wherever it is spoken.

When I cook, I listen online to stations from all over the world and when I eat breakfast, my daily newspaper is the app for a free tabloid I used to read on my commute to work in Geneva. I can follow stories in other countries as they develop and follow live reactions on social media. I am perhaps more immersed now than when I was studying.

There are also many valuable opportunities for learning other languages online. A favourite of my family is *Duolingo* (although some linguists criticised errors in early versions). This tool, available as an app or a website, scaffolds your language learning through purposeful practice and gamification, keeping track of vocabulary and grammar you haven't used for a while or consistently get wrong, and encourages you positively to keep going with your studies.

And if you still want to know more about teaching with digital technologies, there are many workshops and courses available online, often for free. Whether you feel you are a digital immigrant or native, being literate in the modern world is not an option if you are teaching students who are the future. Get yourself up-to-speed, collaborate with colleagues, and seek professional development opportunities to keep on track and online.

Summary

- Make sure there is a good reason to use digital technology in your lesson – always prioritise the educational purpose of what you are doing.

- Decide whether you are using digital technology to enhance or transform what you are teaching – use one of the models provided (SAMR or TECH) to help you with this.

- Digital technologies can bring language learning to life, enlivening exercises and tests grammar and vocabulary, and showcases other cultures in virtual reality or real life.

- Care needs to be taken when using tools that connect to the outside world – follow school policy and seek advice so that students can safely research materials in foreign languages and on websites based in other countries.

- Use digital technology, such as apps, internet radio and social media to reconnect and keep up-to-date with the language you teach – and encourage your students to help you too!

11 Global thinking

What is global thinking?

Global thinking is about learning how to live in a complex world as an active and engaged citizen. It is about considering the bigger picture and appreciating the nature and depth of our shared humanity.

When we encourage global thinking in students we help them recognise, examine and express their own and others' perspectives. We need to scaffold students' thinking to enable them to engage on cognitive, social and emotional levels, and construct their understanding of the world to be able to participate fully in its future.

We as teachers can help students develop routines and habits of mind to enable them to move beyond the familiar, discern that which is of local and global significance, make comparisons, take a cultural perspective and challenge stereotypes. We can encourage them to learn about contexts and traditions, and provide opportunities for them to reflect on their own and others' viewpoints.

Why adopt a global thinking approach?

Global thinking is particularly relevant in an interconnected, digitised world where ideas, opinions and trends are rapidly and relentlessly circulated. Students learn to pause and evaluate. They study why a topic is important on a personal, local and global scale, and they will be motivated to understand the world and their significance in it. Students gain a deeper understanding of why different viewpoints and ideas are held across the world.

Global thinking is something we can nurture both within and across disciplines. We can invite students to learn how to use different lenses from each discipline to see and interpret the world. They also learn how best to apply and communicate key concepts within and across disciplines. We can help our students select the appropriate media and technology to communicate and create their own personal synthesis of the information they have gathered.

Global thinking enables students to become more rounded individuals who perceive themselves as actors in a global context and who value diversity. It encourages them to become more aware, curious and interested in learning about the world and how it works. It helps students to challenge assumptions and stereotypes, to be better informed and more respectful. Global thinking takes the focus beyond exams and grades, or even checklists of skills and attributes. It develops students who are more ready to compete in the global marketplace and more able to participate effectively in an interconnected world.

What are the challenges of incorporating global thinking?

The pressures of an already full curriculum, the need to meet national and local standards, and the demands of exam preparation may make it seem challenging to find time to incorporate global thinking into lessons and programmes of study. A whole-school approach may be required for global thinking to be incorporated in subject plans for teaching and learning.

We need to give all students the opportunity to find their voice and participate actively and confidently, regardless of their background and world experiences, when exploring issues of global significance. We need to design suitable activities that are clear, ongoing and varying. Students need to be able to connect with materials, and extend and challenge their thinking. We also need to devise and use new forms of assessment that incorporate flexible and cooperative thinking.

Opening minds

It is not always a natural step for students of Modern Foreign Languages to be 'global thinkers'. As we have discussed in previous chapters, some may see our subject as just another lesson in their day, detached from real life. Others, even if they enjoy studying languages, may not yet be able to see the wider benefits of what they are learning. It is up to us as teachers to open our students' minds and introduce them to thinking globally.

LESSON IDEA 11.1: STARTER ACTIVITIES USING PRODUCTS

Ask your students to look for labels on anything they are wearing or carrying (e.g. bags, stationery, phones) to see where they were made. You may be lucky and find someone has an item that was manufactured in a country where the language you are teaching is spoken. Alternatively, ask your students to name products – which could be physical or cultural – that native speakers of the language you are teaching have developed. These two 'starter' activities will help your students appreciate better the interconnectedness of the world.

When thinking globally it can be useful, metaphorically, to wear different lenses. This can help our students get into the habit of considering both language and culture.

With limited experience of the world, it is quite normal for students initially to see what they are studying only in the context of themselves as individuals. It may be a while before they come into contact with a speaker of that language so, in the meantime, they will only know countries in which the language is spoken in terms of what is in their textbooks or what others tell them. The longer they study, the easier they will be able to take a broader perspective on what they are learning.

The sooner students can meaningfully put the language they are learning into practice, the better. This will give them greater confidence and encourage them to go further. Help them imagine real life situations where they are role-playing in the language across all four skills. This could take the form of simple conversations, short texts to read or write, or street signs to identify. In addition, make sure your students know where in the world the language is spoken and why.

More advanced students will need to engage more deeply with the language they are learning and the cultures it relates to. Don't be surprised if some students show less interest in the 'mother' country of the language they are studying. As we saw in Chapter 3 **The nature and the subject** and Chapter 4 **Key considerations**, students may be more excited by the fact that the language is spoken in other countries, and this can in fact be a motivator and something to be promoted when thinking globally as a teacher.

Figure 11.1: Knowing a language can be your passport to the world.

Even from a young age, students can quickly begin to appreciate through their learning of languages that other nations and cultures may have alternative perspectives. They will explore why people outside their own country think and act differently on the global stage, be it in politics, arts or sport. And they will begin to recognise why speakers of other languages may give priority to different aspects of their lives or why they react in certain ways when their viewpoint is not the same as ours.

Indeed, this is something that is key for students who are studying a language at an advanced level. When they examine and debate topics such as social interactions, health and the environment, students will need to consider the outlook of other speakers, wherever they live, and do so without prejudice. They will need to seek primary sources of information to know what speakers in a particular community think and feel, sometimes stepping out of their comfort zone to do so.

This in turn helps students put the language they are studying and the culture of those who speak it into perspective. We need not only to nurture students through their own reactions to the topics they meet but also suggest how the reactions of people from other countries might differ. What happens across land borders where languages are not the same, for example, or how do countries with languages in common stick together?

☑ LESSON IDEA ONLINE 11.2: RECOGNISING AND CELEBRATING CULTURAL DIFFERENCES
In this activity, we have used the six official UN languages of Arabic, Chinese, English, French, Russian and Spanish as our focus.

Teacher Tip

Clearly, it is very beneficial for language teachers to share thoughts and strategies with colleagues who teach Humanities subjects. Ask another teacher to give your class an introduction to a topic related to their specialism that you will be teaching (let them choose in which language to present!). Prepare this collaboratively so that learning is scaffolded securely.

Engaging with the world

Students who show a keen interest in and aptitude for learning languages may often see our subject as a passport to their future life. One day they could be working in another country or participating on the world stage. When we lived respectively in the intensely international cities of Brussels and Geneva, we witnessed first-hand the extent to which knowledge of languages and respect for other people's perspectives was essential for the work we were doing.

Figure 11.2: Living and working in an international city can require knowledge of more than one language.

It is usually when students are older and more able to travel independently that they can truly experience a modern foreign language in its own setting. It is likewise only when they have spent some significant time abroad that they can normally look at their own country with some objectivity. In post-16 study, and sooner if they are ready, help your students identify similarities, differences and inter-dependencies by choosing topics of global significance at an appropriate level.

Veronica Boix Mansilla and Anthony Jackson from Harvard University's Graduate School of Education, in their report for the Asia Society Partnership for Global Learning, suggested that topics of global significance should:

- generate deep engagement, through being connected to the reality of students' lives and also allowing a teacher to demonstrate their own passion.

- have clear local–global connections, so that comparisons can be made and impact shown.
- have visible global significance, on multiple grounds, affecting many people and directly affecting students' lives.
- have robust disciplinary and interdisciplinary grounding, using facts to introduce problems and complexities to wrestle with.

⊡ LESSON IDEA ONLINE 11.3: GLOBAL THINKING ROUTINES
Bearing in mind Boix-Mansilla and Jackson's bullet points, try these two interlinked routines to get students started on a topic.

Teacher Tip

To learn more about topics of global significance, take a look at Jean-François Rischard's concise book, *High Noon: 20 Global Problems, 20 Years to Solve Them*.

Students thus engaged with the world become more confident in their own opinions and more reflective in how they consider the opinion of others. This in turn gives them a greater sense of responsibility for their place and role at this time in the history of the world. They are more likely to be inventive in their interactions with people from other linguistic backgrounds and, given the right circumstance, disposed to finding solutions to issues that shape all our lives.

Acting globally

The distinguished educator George Walker said that schools sometimes do not dig deeply enough when encouraging students to gain an appreciation of other cultures. As someone keen on mnemonics, he coded this as 5 'F's and 3 'C's, the former being more superficial than the latter.

Flags	Communicating
Festivals	
Food	Collaborating
Fashion	
Famous people	Critical thinking

Figure 11.3

The items listed in the left-hand column of Figure 11.3 have their place, particularly when motivating younger students. It is in fact quite fun, even as an adult, to consider the 5 'F's and a nice end-of-term way to celebrate with your students aspects of the language you are teaching. Famous people who speak other languages can be, as we have shown, a valuable attraction. But it is the elements on the right-hand column that give greater depth to students' understanding of the world and their ability to act globally.

LESSON IDEA 11.4: THE 5 'F'S

Ask your students to research, in groups, the 5 'F's for the language they are studying. This works particularly well if the language is spoken in more than one country.

Figure 11.4: The flagpole entrance to the UN base in Geneva, Switzerland.

How can we lead students towards communicating, collaborating and thinking critically in another language and about the countries where that language is spoken? Once again, a staged approach is best. Students in lower levels will be well aware that they do not know enough vocabulary and grammar to talk or write about everything in a foreign language to the extent that they may do in their own language. We need to give them the building blocks and tools.

Younger students will enjoy expanding their vocabulary by creating simple sentences. Advanced students need to work on creating clear statements and combining these together using appropriate grammar. In many languages, this involves using more complex grammar, such as the subjunctive mood. You will need to decide how best to plan this. What do you do first? Do you teach the grammar point or, to give students an opportunity to think harder, do you get them to spot that something has changed?

When students are thinking critically about topics of global significance, they have to express opinions. They may struggle to do this in their own language and, depending on their disposition, this may make it easier or harder for them to do so in a foreign language. They will certainly need to widen their pool of adjectives: not everything can be qualified as 'interesting' or 'boring' when they reach this level!

LESSON IDEA 11.5: EXPRESSING OPINIONS

Put students into pairs. One student has to express an opinion, whether they agree with it or not, and the other has to express the opposite (doing more than simply turning the same phrase into a negative or positive!). This will aid both in the expansion of vocabulary and in the formation of viewpoints. What gets written (once checked) can then become material for other students to review and use.

Such an exercise follows what we suggested in Chapter 6 **Active learning**. Teachers facilitate learning but more advanced students need to form the habits to explore the world on their own. You cannot tell them what to think about a particular topic but you can give them the structures and routines to discover their own perspectives. The more they communicate and collaborate with each other on this, the more readily they will be able to do it.

Teacher Tip

Make sure you know the latest vocabulary for the topics you are teaching. New technologies and diseases are discovered and words go in and out of fashion. Keep yourself up-to-date by setting aside time to read or listen to articles on current affairs in the language you teach.

Students at IGCSE level can also be encouraged to think globally, even if we are not yet asking them to express their opinions on topics of global significance. They will be communicating in the foreign language about themes such as their holidays, where they live or their families. To stretch and challenge them, ask them to imagine their audience to be native speakers and therefore to make comparisons or include any cultural differences of which they are aware.

This is where food and festivals are fertile ground. Students can demonstrate their understanding of the culture of a country where a language is spoken by talking about what is eaten there, what special days there are in their calendar and how they are celebrated. Location and domestic situations are likewise worth knowing about in some detail even at IGCSE. Do people live in houses or apartments? Do they live in extended families? Do they have pets or working animals?

Being global

In 1996, UNESCO published a report by Jacques Delors called *Learning: The Treasure Within*. This report is widely considered to be a key reference for the conceptualisation of education and learning worldwide. It is based on 'four key pillars underlying education and life' that have been regularly revisited since and set out a useful paradigm for considering how we might summarise what global thinking means for our students and for us as teachers.

The four pillars are stated and described as:

- **Learning to know** – allowing individuals to gain the basic skills to benefit from educational opportunities that arise throughout life.

- **Learning to do** – allowing individuals to gain the skills to apply what they have learnt to situations outside formal learning.
- **Learning to be** – encouraging individuals to take responsibility for the attainment of goals shared by our common humanity.
- **Learning to live together** – encouraging individuals to understand others, their history, their traditions and their spirituality.

Throughout this book, we have written about the importance of creating the conditions for learning to take place. This is the fundamental and recurrent theme behind all of the approaches set out in each of the chapters. As teachers, it is our duty to set students up for success, to help them learn from their mistakes and to give them opportunities for purposeful practice in their pursuit of gaining mastery of the modern foreign language they are studying.

Teacher Tip

As we reach the end of this book, take time to reflect on to what extent you are creating the conditions for learning to take place in your classroom each day with reference to Delors' four pillars.

Every day we read, hear, say or write things we have never done before. Our reaction is not usually one of disbelief or panic but rather we flounder intelligently, as Professor Guy Claxton expresses it. We have gained the skills and the tools to know how to adapt to new situations. We have learnt them from other people or our own teachers and from the experiences we have been afforded during our lives. It is incumbent on us to do the same for the students in our care.

Linguists tend to have a more rounded way of looking at the world than those who can only express themselves or access materials in one language. It is easy for us to take a global perspective and be less isolationist in our approach to life. We have seen our own country and people through the eyes of others and we have been able to engage with them where ideas converge or diverge, and learnt to appreciate in greater depth the world that we share.

Figure 11.5: Taking a global perspective.

The place of our subject in a school's curriculum is an interesting one. Much of what we cover is a repeat of what students may have seen elsewhere in their education in their own language. They will already know how to talk about who they are and where they are from but will have done so using other words and grammar. If they continue to advanced study of the foreign language, they may paradoxically be asked to express viewpoints on topics they have never previously considered.

To return to one of the themes of our opening chapter about the 'nature' of the subject, Modern Foreign Languages enhance a great deal of what students learn elsewhere at school. Our subject opens new doors to those who need a new challenge or those who have struggled; it provides an extra dimension for those who are specialising in other disciplines, such as the Sciences; and it gives students the keys to a world of discovery in new environments.

Thinking globally, the study of Modern Foreign Languages encourages knowledge, skills and attributes that are useful for life. Even a limited amount of vocabulary or some key phrases can make a difference to an individual's capacity to socialise or work with others, or even survive. As teachers of Modern Foreign Languages, we should regularly remind ourselves of the global picture and all that an understanding of Modern Foreign Languages can bring.

Summary

- Students will not automatically think globally: scaffold their learning to encourage them to take a wider perspective.

- When they are ready, get students to think critically about their own perspectives on the world as well as those of other cultures.

- Establish habits and routines for thinking globally.

- Collaborate with colleagues, particularly those who teach Humanities, when you are considering topics of global significance with your students.

- Encourage students to understand their place in the world and give them the tools to participate as effectively as possible.

12 | Reflective practice

Dr Paul Beedle, Head of Professional Development Qualifications, Cambridge International

'As a teacher you are always learning'

It is easy to say this, isn't it? Is it true? Are you bound to learn just by being a teacher?

You can learn every day from the experience of working with your students, collaborating with your colleagues and playing your part in the life of your school. You can learn also by being receptive to new ideas and approaches, and by applying and evaluating these in practice in your own context.

To be more precise, let us say that as a teacher:

* you **should** always be learning
  to develop your expertise throughout your career for your own fulfilment as a member of the teaching profession and to be as effective as possible in the classroom.
* you **can** always be learning
  if you approach the teaching experience with an open mind, ready to learn and knowing how to reflect on what you are doing in order to improve.

You want your professional development activities to be as relevant as possible to what you do and who you are, and to help change the quality of your teaching and your students' learning – for the better, in terms of outcomes, and for good, in terms of lasting effect. You want to feel that 'it all makes sense' and that you are actively following a path that works for you personally, professionally and career-wise.

So professional learning is about making the most of opportunities and your working environment, bearing in mind who you are, what you are like and how you want to improve. But simply experiencing – thinking about and responding to situations, and absorbing ideas and information – is not necessarily learning. It is through reflection that you can make the most of your experience to deepen and extend your professional skills and understanding.

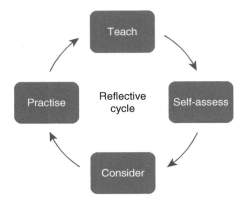

Figure 12.1

In this chapter, we will focus on three *essentials* of reflective practice, explaining in principle and in practice how you can support your own continuing professional development:

1 **Focusing** on what you want to learn about and why.
2 **Challenging** yourself and others to go beyond description and assumptions to critical analysis and evaluation.
3 **Sharing** what you are learning with colleagues – to enrich understanding and enhance the quality of practice.

These essentials will help you as you apply and adapt the rich ideas and approaches in this book in your own particular context. They will also help you if you are, or are about to be, taking part in a Cambridge Professional Development Qualification (Cambridge PDQ) programme, to make the most of your programme, develop your portfolio and gain the qualification.

1 Focus
In principle

Given the multiple dimensions and demands of being a teacher, you might be tempted to try to cover 'everything' in your professional development but you will then not have the time to go beneath the surface much at all. Likewise, attending many different training events will certainly keep you very busy but it is unlikely that these will simply add up to improving your thinking and practice in sustainable and systematic ways.

Teachers who are beginning an organised programme of professional learning find that it is most helpful to select particular ideas, approaches and topics which are relevant to their own situation and their school's priorities. They can then be clear about their professional learning goals, and how their own learning contributes to improving their students' learning outcomes. They deliberately choose activities that help make sense of their practice with their students in their school and have a clear overall purpose.

It is one thing achieving focus, and another maintaining this over time. When the going gets tough, because it is difficult either to understand or become familiar with new ideas and practices, or to balance learning time with the demands of work and life, it really helps to have a mission – to know why you want to learn something as well as what that something is. Make sure that this is a purpose which you feel genuinely belongs to you and in which you have a keen interest, rather than it being something given to you or imposed on you. Articulate your focus not just by writing it down but by 'pitching' it to a colleague whose opinion you trust and taking note of their feedback.

In practice

- Plan
  What is my goal and how will I approach the activity?

  Select an approach that is new to you, but make sure that you understand the thinking behind this and that it is relevant to your students' learning. Do it for real effect, not for show.

- Monitor
  Am I making progress towards my goal; do I need to try a different approach?

  Take time during your professional development programme to review how far and well you are developing your understanding of theory and practice. What can you do to get more out of the experience, for example by discussing issues with your mentor, researching particular points, and asking your colleagues for their advice?

- Evaluate
  What went well, what could have been better, what have I learned for next time?

  Evaluation can sometimes be seen as a 'duty to perform' – like clearing up after the event – rather than the pivotal moment in learning that it really is. Evaluate not because you are told you have to; evaluate to make sense of the learning experience you have been through and what it means to you, and to plan ahead to see what you can do in the future.

This cycle of planning, monitoring and evaluation is just as relevant to you as a professional learner as to your students as learners. Be actively in charge of your learning and take appropriate actions. Make your professional development work for you. Of course your professional development programme leaders, trainers and mentors will guide and support you in your learning, but you are at the heart of your own learning experience, not on the receiving end of something that is cast in stone. Those who assist and advise you on your professional development want you and your colleagues to get the best out of the experience, and need your feedback along the way so that if necessary they can adapt and improve what they are devising.

2 Challenge

In principle

Reflection is a constructive process that helps the individual teacher to improve their thinking and practice. It involves regularly asking questions of yourself about your developing ideas and experience, and keeping track of your developing thinking, for example in a reflective journal. Reflection is continuous, rather than a one-off experience. Being honest with yourself means thinking hard, prompting yourself to go beyond your first thoughts about a new experience and to avoid taking for granted your opinions about something to which you are accustomed. Be a critical friend to yourself.

In the Cambridge PDQ Certificate in Teaching and Learning, for example, teachers take a fresh look at the concepts and processes of learning and challenge their own assumptions. They engage with theory and models of effective teaching and learning, and open their minds through observing experienced practitioners, applying new ideas in practice and listening to formative feedback from mentors and colleagues. To evidence in their assessed portfolio how they have learned from this experience, they not only present records of observed practice but also critical analysis showing understanding of how and why practices work and how they can be put into different contexts successfully.

The Cambridge PDQ syllabuses set out key questions to focus professional learning and the portfolio templates prompts to help you. These questions provide a framework for reflection. They are open-ended and will not only stimulate your thinking but lead to lively group discussion. The discipline of asking yourself and others questions such as 'Why?' 'How do we know?' 'What is the evidence?' 'What are the conditions?' leads to thoughtful and intelligent practice.

In practice

Challenge:

- Yourself, as you reflect on an experience, to be more critical in your thinking. For example, rather than simply describing what happened, analyse why it happened and its significance, and what might have happened if conditions had been different.
- Theory – by understanding and analysing the argument, and evaluating the evidence that supports the theory. Don't simply accept a theory as a given fact – be sure that you feel that the ideas make sense and that there is positive value in applying them in practice.
- Convention – the concept of 'best practice(s)' is as good as we know now, on the basis of the body of evidence, for example on the effect size of impact of a particular approach on learning outcomes (defined in the next chapter). By using an approach in an informed way and with a critical eye, you can evaluate the approach relating to your particular situation.

3 Share

In principle

Schools are such busy places, and yet teachers can feel they are working on their own for long periods because of the intensity of their workload as they focus on all that is involved in teaching their students. We know that a crucial part of our students' active learning is the opportunity to collaborate with their peers in order to investigate, create and communicate. Just so with professional learning: teachers learn best through engagement with their peers, in their own school and beyond. Discussion and interaction with colleagues, focused on learning and student outcomes, and carried out in a culture of openness, trust and respect, helps each member of the community of practice in the school clarify and sharpen their understanding and enhance their practice.

This is why the best professional learning programmes incorporate collaborative learning, and pivotal moments are designed into the programme for this to happen frequently over time: formally in guided learning sessions such as workshops and more informally in opportunities such as study group, teach meets and discussion, both face-to-face and online.

In practice

Go beyond expectations!

In the Cambridge PDQ syllabus, each candidate needs to carry out an observation of an experienced practitioner and to be observed formatively themselves by their mentor on a small number of occasions. This is the formal requirement in terms of evidence of practice within the portfolio for the qualification. The expectation is that these are not the only times that teachers will observe and be observed for professional learning purposes (rather than performance appraisal).

However, the more that teachers can observe each other's teaching, the better; sharing of practice leads to advancement of shared knowledge and understanding of aspects of teaching and learning, and development of agreed shared 'best practice'.

So:

- open your classroom door to observation
- share with your closest colleague(s) when you are trying out a fresh approach, such as an idea in this book
- ask them to look for particular aspects in the lesson, especially how students are engaging with the approach – pose an observation question
- reflect with them after the lesson on what you and they have learned from the experience – pose an evaluation question
- go and observe them as they do the same
- after a number of lessons, discuss with your colleagues how you can build on your peer observation with common purpose (for example, lesson study)
- share with your other colleagues in the school what you are gaining from this collaboration and encourage them to do the same
- always have question(s) to focus observations and focus these question(s) on student outcomes.

Pathways

The short-term effects of professional development are very much centred on teachers' students. For example, the professional learning in a Cambridge PDQ programme should lead directly and quickly to changes in the ways your students learn. All teachers have this at heart – the desire to help their students learn better.

The long-term effects of professional development are more teacher-centric. During their career over, say, 30 years, a teacher may teach many thousand lessons. There are many good reasons for a teacher to keep up-to-date with pedagogy, not least to sustain their enjoyment of what they do.

Each teacher will follow their own career pathway, taking into account many factors. We do work within systems, at school and wider level, involving salary and appointment levels, and professional development can be linked to these as requirement or expectation. However, to a significant extent teachers shape their own career pathway, making decisions along the way. Their pathway is not pre-ordained; there is room for personal choice, opportunity and serendipity. It is for each teacher to judge for themselves how much they wish to venture. A teacher's professional development pathway should reflect and support this.

It is a big decision to embark on an extended programme of professional development, involving a significant commitment of hours of learning and preparation over several months. You need to be as clear as you can be about the immediate and long-term value of such a commitment. Will your programme lead to academic credit as part of a stepped pathway towards Masters level, for example?

Throughout your career, you need to be mindful of the opportunities you have for professional development. Gauge the value of options available at each particular stage in your professional life, both in terms of relevance to your current situation – your students, subject and phase focus, and school – and the future situation(s) of which you are thinking.

13 Understanding the impact of classroom practice on student progress

Lee Davis, Deputy Director for Education, Cambridge International

Introduction

Throughout this book, you have been encouraged to adopt a more active approach to teaching and learning and to ensure that formative assessment is embedded into your classroom practice. In addition, you have been asked to develop your students as meta-learners, such that they are able to, as the academic Chris Watkins puts it, 'narrate their own learning' and become more reflective and strategic in how they plan, carry out and then review any given learning activity.

A key question remains, however. How will you know that the new strategies and approaches you intend to adopt have made a significant difference to your students' progress and learning? What, in other words, has been the impact and how will you know?

This chapter looks at how you might go about determining this at the classroom level. It deliberately avoids reference to whole-school student tracking systems, because these are not readily available to all schools and all teachers. Instead, it considers what you can do as an individual teacher to make the learning of your students visible – both to you and anyone else who is interested in how they are doing. It does so by introducing the concept of 'effect sizes' and shows how these can be used by teachers to determine not just whether an intervention works or not but, more importantly, *how well* it works. 'Effect size' is a useful way of quantifying or measuring the size of any difference between two groups or data sets. The aim is to place emphasis on the most important aspect of an intervention or change in teaching approach – the **size of the effect** on student outcomes.

Consider the following scenario:

Over the course of a term, a teacher has worked hard with her students on understanding 'what success looks like' for any given task or activity. She has stressed the importance of everyone being clear about the criteria for success, before students embark upon the chosen task and plan their way through it. She has even got to the point where students have been co-authors of the assessment rubrics used, so that they have been fully engaged in the intended outcomes throughout and can articulate what is required before they have even started. The teacher is happy with developments so far, but has it made a difference to student progress? Has learning increased beyond what we would normally expect for an average student over a term anyway?

Here is an extract from the teacher's markbook.

Student	Sept Task	Nov Task
Katya	13	15
Maria	15	20
Joao	17	23
David	20	18
Mushtaq	23	25
Caio	25	38
Cristina	28	42
Tom	30	35
Hema	32	37
Jennifer	35	40

Figure 13.1

Before we start analysing this data, we must note the following:

* The task given in September was at the start of the term – the task in November was towards the end of the term.
* Both tasks assessed similar skills, knowledge and understanding in the student.
* The maximum mark for each was 50.
* The only variable that has changed over the course of the term is the approaches to teaching and learning by the teacher. All other things are equal.

With that in mind, looking at Figure 13.1, what conclusions might you draw as an external observer?

You might be saying something along the lines of: 'Mushtaq and Katya have made some progress, but not very much. Caio and Cristina appear to have done particularly well. David, on the other hand, appears to be going backwards!'

What can you say about the class as a whole?

Calculating effect sizes

What if we were to apply the concept of 'effect sizes' to the class results in Figure 13.1, so that we could make some more definitive statements about the impact of the interventions over the given time period? Remember, we are doing so in order to understand the size of the effect on student outcomes or progress.

Let's start by understanding how it is calculated.

An effect size is found by calculating 'the standardised mean difference between two data sets or groups'. In essence, this means we are looking for the difference between two averages, while taking into the account the spread of values (in this case, marks) around those averages at the same time.

As a formula, and from Figure 13.1, it looks like the following:

$$\text{Effect size} = \frac{\text{average class mark (after intervention)} - \text{average class mark (before intervention)}}{\text{spread (standard deviation of the class)}}$$

In words: the average mark achieved by the class *before* the teacher introduced her intervention strategies is taken away from the average mark achieved by the class *after* the intervention strategies. This is then divided by the standard deviation[1] of the class as a whole.

---

[1] The standard deviation is merely a way of expressing by how much the members of a group (in this case, student marks in the class) differ from the average value (or mark) for the group.

Inserting our data into a spreadsheet helps us calculate the effect size as follows:

	A	B	C
1	**Student**	September Task	November Task
2	Katya	13	15
3	Maria	15	20
4	Joao	17	23
5	David	20	18
6	Mushtaq	23	25
7	Caio	25	38
8	Cristina	28	42
9	Tom	30	35
10	Hema	32	37
11	Jennifer	35	40
12			
13	Average mark	23.8 = AVERAGE (B2:B11)	29.3 = AVERAGE (C2:C11)
14	Standard deviation	7.5 = STDEV (B2:B11)	10.11 = STDEV (C2:C11)

Figure 13.2

Therefore, the effect size for this class $= \dfrac{29.3 - 23.8}{8.8} = 0.62$
But what does this mean?

Interpreting effect sizes for classroom practice

In pure statistical terms, a 0.62 effect size means that the average student mark **after** the intervention by the teacher, is 0.62 standard deviations above the average student mark **before** the intervention.

We can state this in another way: the post-intervention average mark now exceeds 61% of the student marks previously.

Going further, we can also say that the average student mark, post-intervention, would have placed a student in the top four in the class previously. You can see this visually in Figure 13.2 where 29.3 (the class average after the teacher's interventions) would have been between Cristina's and Tom's marks in the September task.

This is good, isn't it? As a teacher, would you be happy with this progress by the class over the term?

To help understand effect sizes further, and therefore how well or otherwise the teacher has done above, let us look at how they are used in large-scale studies as well as research into educational effectiveness more broadly. We will then turn our attention to what really matters – talking about student learning.

Effect sizes in research

We know from results analyses of the Program for International Student Assessment (PISA) and the Trends in International Mathematics and Science Study (TIMMS) that, across the world, a year's schooling leads to an effect size of 0.4. John Hattie and his team at The University of Melbourne reached similar conclusions when looking at over 900 meta-analyses of classroom and whole-school interventions to improve student learning – 240 million students later, the result was an effect size of 0.4 on average for all these strategies.

What this means, then, is that any teacher achieving an effect size of greater than 0.4 is doing better than expected (than the average) over the course of a year. From our earlier example, not only are the students making better than expected progress, they are also doing so in just one term.

Here is something else to consider. In England, the distribution of GCSE grades in Maths and English have standard deviations of between 1.5 and 1.8 grades (A★, A, B, C, etc.), so an improvement of one GCSE grade represents an effect size of between 0.5 and 0.7. This means that, in the context of secondary schools, introducing a change in classroom practice of 0.62 (as the teacher achieved above) would result in an improvement of about one GCSE grade for each student in the subject.

Furthermore, for a school in which 50% of students were previously attaining five or more A★–C grades, this percentage (assuming the effect size of 0.62 applied equally across all subjects and all other things being equal) would rise to 73%.

Now, that's something worth knowing.

What next for your classroom practice? Talking about student learning

Given what we now know about 'effect sizes', what might be the practical next steps for you as a teacher?

Firstly, try calculating 'effect sizes' for yourself, using marks and scores for your students that are comparable, e.g. student performance on key skills in Maths, Reading, Writing, Science practicals, etc. Become familiar with how they are calculated so that you can then start interrogating them 'intelligently'.

Do the results indicate progress was made? If so, how much is attributable to the interventions you have introduced?

Try calculating 'effect sizes' for each individual student, in addition to your class, to make their progress visible too. To help illustrate this, let us return to the comments we were making about the progress of some students in Figure 13.1. We thought Cristina and Caio did very well and we had grave concerns about David. Individual effect sizes for the class of students would help us shed light on this further:

Student	September Task	November task	Individual Effect Size
Katya	13	15	0.22*
Maria	15	20	0.55
Joao	17	23	0.66
David	20	18	-0.22
Mushtaq	23	25	0.22
Caio	25	38	1.43
Cristina	28	42	1.54
Tom	30	35	0.55
Hema	32	37	0.55
Jennifer	35	40	0.55

* The individual 'effect size' for each student above is calculated by taking their September mark away from their November mark and then dividing by the standard deviation for the class – in this case, 8.8.

Figure 13.3

If these were your students, what questions would you now ask of yourself, of your students and even of your colleagues, to help you understand why the results are as they are and how learning is best achieved? Remember, an effect size of 0.4 is our benchmark, so who is doing better than that? Who is not making the progress we would expect?

David's situation immediately stands out, doesn't it? A negative effect size implies learning has regressed. So, what has happened, and how will we draw alongside him to find out what the issues are and how best to address them?

Why did Caio and Cristina do so well, considering they were just above average previously? Effect sizes of 1.43 and 1.54 respectively are significantly above the benchmark, so what has changed from their perspective? Perhaps they responded particularly positively to developing assessment rubrics together. Perhaps learning had sometimes been a mystery to them before, but with success criteria now made clear, this obstacle to learning had been removed.

We don't know the answers to these questions, but they would be great to ask, wouldn't they? So go ahead and ask them. Engage in dialogue with your students, and see how their own ability to discuss their learning has changed and developed. This will be as powerful a way as any of discovering whether your new approaches to teaching and learning have had an impact and it ultimately puts data, such as 'effect sizes', into context.

Concluding remarks

'Effect sizes' are a very effective means of helping you understand the impact of your classroom practice upon student progress. If you change your teaching strategies in some way, calculating 'effect sizes', for both the class and each individual student, helps you determine not just *if* learning has improved, but by *how much*.

They are, though, only part of the process. As teachers, we must look at the data carefully and intelligently in order to understand 'why'. Why did some students do better than others? Why did some not make any progress at all? Use 'effect sizes' as a starting point, not the end in itself.

Ensure that you don't do this in isolation – collaborate with others and share this approach with them. What are your colleagues finding in their classes, in their subjects? Are the same students making the same progress across the curriculum? If there are differences, what might account for them?

In answering such questions, we will be in a much better position to determine next steps in the learning process for students. After all, isn't that our primary purpose as teachers?

Acknowledgements, further reading and resources

This chapter has drawn extensively on the influential work of the academics John Hattie and Robert Coe. You are encouraged to look at the following resources to develop your understanding further:

Hattie, J. (2012) *Visible Learning for Teachers – Maximising Impact on Learning*. London and New York: Routledge.

Coe, R. (2002) *It's the Effect Size, Stupid. What effect size is and why it is important.* Paper presented at the Annual Conference of The British Educational Research Association, University of Exeter, England, 12–14 September, 2002. A version of the paper is available online on the University of Leeds website.

The Centre for Evaluation and Monitoring, University of Durham, has produced a very useful 'effect size' calculator (available from their website). Note that it also calculates a confidence interval for any 'effect size' generated. Confidence intervals are useful in helping you understand the margin for error of an 'effect size' you are reporting for your class. These are particularly important when the sample size is small, which will inevitably be the case for most classroom teachers.

14 Recommended reading

For a deeper understanding of the Cambridge approach, refer to the Cambridge International website (http://www.cambridgeinternational.org/teaching-and-learning) where you will find the following resources:

Implementing the curriculum with Cambridge: a guide for school leaders.

Developing your school with Cambridge: a guide for school leaders.

Education Briefs for a number of topics, such as active learning and bilingual education. Each brief includes information about the challenges and benefits of different approaches to teaching, practical tips, lists of resources.

Getting started with ... These are interactive resources to help explore and develop areas of teaching and learning. They include practical examples, reflective questions, and experiences from teachers and researchers.

For further support around becoming a Cambridge school, visit cambridge-community.org.uk.

The resources in this section can be used as a supplement to your learning, to build upon your awareness of Modern Foreign Languages teaching and the pedagogical themes in this series.

Chapter 4
Perkins, D. (2014) *Future Wise: Educating our Children for a Changing World.* San Francisco: Jossey-Bass.

Chapter 6
Hattie, J. (2011) *Visible Learning for Teachers.* Abingdon, UK: Routledge.

Chapter 7
Clarke, S. (2014) *Outstanding Formative Assessment: Culture and Practice.* Abingdon: Hodder Education.

Wiliam, D. (2011) *Embedded Formative Assessment.* Bloomington: Solution Tree.

Chapter 11
Kathy, S. (2017) Online, *Guide to Everything* (Kathy Schrock's Guide to Everything website).

Roberts, J. (2017) Online, *Teaching literacy with technology in an era of educational innovation. By Jen Roberts@JenRoberts* (Literacy, Technology, Policy, Etc....A Blog website).

Chapter 12
Rischard, J. F. (2000) *High Noon: 20 Global Problems, 20 Years to Solve Them*. US: Basic Books.

Delors, J. *et al.* (1996) Online, *Learning: The Treasure Within: Report to UNESCO of the International Commission on Education for the Twenty-first Century* (UNESCO Publishing website).

Boix-Mansilla, V. and Jackson, A. (2014) Online, *Educating for Global Competence: Preparing Our Youth to Engage the World* (Asia Society Partnership for Global Learning website).

Chapter 14
Watkins, C. (2015) *Meta-Learning in Classrooms*. The SAGE Handbook of Learning. Edited by Scott D. and Hargreaves E. London: Sage Publications.

Index

Approaches to learning and teaching Modern Foreign Languages

Kaizena, 100
KWL chart, 66

language generation, 66–67
language skills, 12–13
learning evaluation, 72–73
learning, evidence of, 53
    questions, 53–55
learning journals, 73
learning targets, 50–51

metacognition
    challenges, 64
    defined, 62–63
    developing linguists, 65
    feedback, 71
    importance of, 63
    learning evaluation, 72–73
    learning goal, 65
    modelling strategies,
        67–68
    monitoring progress,
        69–70
    phases involved in, 62–63
    planning, 65
    skills, 63–64
modelling strategies, 67–68

modern foreign language, key
    considerations, 17–22
    basics of, 17–18
    essentials, 19–22
    future, 17–18
Modern Foreign Languages.
    See foreign languages
monitoring progress, 69–71

online testing programmes, 99

photos and videos, 99
predicting, 66
prior learning, 65–66
programme of study, 27–29
progressive mind
    mapping, 44

questioning, 38–40

reflective practice, professional
    development, 119–125
    challenging, 122–123
    focusing, 120–122
    long-term effects, 125
    sharing, 123–124
    short-term effects, 124

SAMR. See Substitute,
    Augmentation,
    Modification,
    Redefinition (SAMR)
Seesaw, 99
smartphones and tablets, 98–99
social media, 100–101
Substitute, Augmentation,
    Modification, Redefinition
    (SAMR), 95–96
success criteria, identifying, 52
syllabus, 25–27
    beyond the, 30–32
    planning, 27–32

target language, 17
TECH. See Traditional,
    Enhanced, Choice,
    Handoff (TECH)
textbooks, 14, 20, 29
thinking skill, 39
Traditional, Enhanced, Choice,
    Handoff (TECH), 96

virtual reality, 99–100

websites and apps, 99, 100

140